THIS BOOK BELONGS TO
The Library of

....

....

I can't tell you how grateful I am that you decided to read my book. My most heartfelt thanks that you took time out of your life to choose my work and I hope you find benefit within these pages.

There are so many books available today that offer similar content so that makes it even more humbling that you decided to buying mine.

Tell me what you thought! I am eager to hear your opinion and ideas on what you read as are others who are looking for a good book to buy. Leave a review on Amazon.com so others can benefit from your wisdom!

With much thanks.

Table of Contents

INTRODUCTION

Taking Charge of Your Own Future

"If you can't you must, and if you must you can." –Tony Robbins
What was your key lesson from the year 2021? Mine was that humans are resilient and creative, and we're able to adapt to anything life throws at us. But also, that e-Commerce as a business model is necessary and will continue to be a fundamental aspect of consumer shopping, and if you want to be successful at it, you must read this book from cover to cover. Well, more importantly, you must apply the key teachings I'll be sharing in it, to your business.

E-Commerce is getting more difficult to navigate. There are literally millions of e-Commerce stores on the web from all parts of the world. Most countries can ship products internationally (some have digital products, so they don't even have to ship anything), they're able to pay for Google and Meta ads (I think we can call them "Meta ads" now, since the company introduced the name change months ago at the time of this writing, and Facebook and Instagram ads can be run under one dashboard), and most marketers and business owners are starting to understand the concept and functionality of social media, and applying it to their businesses. Your e-Commerce store has got to do more than just stand out.

You have to bring about an amazing customer experience, from the moment consumers first hear about or see your brand, to the point beyond their first purchase. They have to be mesmerized by how you do things. Just having a website with products and a payment gateway isn't going to cut it; simply posting about your products on Instagram or running a few conversion ads on Facebook won't, either. Everyone is already doing that. Now, it's not like you can do anything else—there isn't a better way to get traffic other than social and digital media, and converting customers through website sales (rather than social selling) is still your best shot.

However, the 'how' is more important than the 'what.' How you do things has to be different, interesting, captivating—I don't think I need to add any more adjectives for you to get this. After all, you've been living it. You've seen how your social media content and ads aren't converting. You've seen how your website isn't getting much traffic and even when you do have a few views, the bounce rate is something to cry about. But I'm so glad you haven't quit just yet and decided, instead, to pick up this book.

As the son of two entrepreneurs, I've always felt like entrepreneurship was in my blood, and used the skills I've observed from my parents to leverage the internet to make money. When I first started making money online, I was drawn into the amount of sheer potential available on the net, right in the palm of anyone's hand. I've since developed a passion for helping people live life with the courage to do what they want to do, and also helping them make more informed financial decisions about their life. One way they could do so is by investing their money into an e-Commerce business, which will help them generate more profits and larger returns over time.

I'll be sharing information on how you can start an e-Commerce business from scratch or optimize the one you already have. So wherever you are in your journey, you'll get the information you need to thrive. Each chapter also has a story of someone possibly in your shoes for you to get inspired. In the first chapter, I'll go over the fundamentals of starting an e-Commerce business, including which platforms to use, and any prerequisites you should be aware of. If you already have an e-Commerce business set up, you can skip over this and move onto Chapter 2.

Chapter 2 is where I highlight the different business models you can use and the pros and cons for each. The one you choose will largely depend on your resources, and perhaps objectives (some of you might want to build a legacy that you can pass down to your grandkids, others may want a way to earn passive income). I'll also help you figure out your niche, how to put together a customer avatar, and which products you can start with.

In the third chapter, I provide you with the key to setting up sales funnels that you can automate. This means you only have to set them up once, and they'll be running automatically, while you focus on other business operations. Yes, you still have to check in on those automations, see if there's anything else you can improve, or switch things up if they don't convert like they used to.

How you're going to get potential customers flooding your online store is discussed in-depth in Chapter 4. Social media and digital platforms are here to stay; what you need to do is find ways to become even better at them—as many ways as you can. I'll also share with you the easiest Facebook ads strategy, which you just have to try.

The final chapter is about amplifying profits, scaling up, optimizing sales and content even further, and outsourcing. I'll also touch on the importance of brand building, now that you're making enough profits to invest in marketing campaigns to drive engagement and stir up conversations, not just sales.

Life and business coach, Tony Robbins, once said "Knowledge isn't power, only potential power." True power comes from applying what you've learned. I want you to go through each of these chapters step-by-step, and apply what you learn. From my experience, people who read through an entire book with the assumption that they'll remember all they've read, tend to get overwhelmed and quit on themselves. But I've got a good feeling that you're not a quitter, and you're ready to take your e-Commerce business idea to the next level.

CHAPTER 1

What You Were Supposed to Know Yesterday

"A brand for a company is like a reputation for a person. You earn reputation by trying to do hard things well." –Jeff Bezos

Starting an e-Commerce business is often viewed as the get-rich-quick method of businesses; nothing more than a great way to earn 'passive' income, and particularly, make tons of money without working hard for it. If this is your impression of it, I'm sorry to have to tell you this: You're wrong. If that was the only reason why you wanted to get into e-Commerce, you need to know that that mentality won't get you far in this line of business. There's a lot of work that goes into setting up an e-Commerce business, regardless of the business model you choose (which I'll discuss in Chapter 2). Although you're able to eventually earn passive income through certain e-Commerce models, you still have to set up a strong foundation for your business.

According to business blogger, Ivan Widjaya, there are several prerequisites to starting an e-Commerce business, including: A great name, a good hosting platform, the right licenses and structures, as well as software and tools to automate your journey. I agree with all of these, and would like to add one more thing: You'll need a bit of working capital to get you started. Within this chapter, I will explain to you what I mean by e-Commerce, briefly cover the importance of a great name and brand design as a whole, how to get the correct licenses, and why you'll need some money to get started.

What Is E-Commerce?

Most people's idea of e-Commerce is the sale of physical products through an online platform. This, however, is only one example of e-Commerce, and although it is what I'll be covering in the rest of the book, I want to make you aware that e-Commerce involves so much more. As explained by author Martin Kutz, "electronic commerce or e-Commerce [refers to] the trading of products or services using computer networks, such as the Internet. Electronic commerce draws on technologies such as mobile commerce, electronic funds transfer, supply chain management, Internet marketing, online transaction processing, electronic data interchange (EDI), inventory management systems, and automated data collection systems (2016, p. 15).

As such, any exchange of physical goods, digital goods, and intellectual services that occur as a result of these processes and technologies can be regarded as e-Commerce. But, as mentioned, I will only be focusing on the selling of physical products. Even if your business idea has a different focus—like services, for instance—you can still apply the core teachings from this book to your business. The formula for business success will always be the same and can be structured over any business model or category. So, use the examples I share, and see how you can apply them to your own e-Commerce business.

Product Research

Some of you reading this book may already have a business idea in mind and you have a solid understanding of what you want to sell. But for those who don't, product research can be rather intimidating, so I want to simplify it for you. Start with what you're passionate about or a real-world problem that you've wanted to solve (or have solved already, for yourself). Business, regardless of the industry, is always going to be difficult; but if you're passionate about your business, you'll be able to overcome any obstacle that stands in your way. Also, understand that passions can grow, so it may be that you're not interested in a particular product as much, but you may learn to love it and what it does for your intended customers. A lot of people have this idea that passion is innate, and that you have to wait for a sign from the universe to tell you what your passion ought to be. But the truth is, we decide what we're going to be passionate about, and what we'll devote our time, resources, and energy to. So, even if you're not clear on your passions or the product you want to sell, understand that you can pick something (almost anything) and fall in love with it.

Next, you want to decide on a niche market. Knowing that you're passionate about health or fashion is one thing, but that is far too broad, and you will want to get more focused. A niche market is basically a subset or segment of the broad category. Health isn't a niche, but supplements that boost health, for instance, is one. In the same light, fashion isn't a niche, but high-fashion sneakers certainly is. Now, unless you have a large budget, it would also be advisable that you start with one product (or a category of products) before you expand. As you sell these products, this not only gives you sufficient proof that you're on the right track, but this can help give you some capital to boost your business.

Now, how do you decide which product or products to start with? Focus on what's trending. Not in terms of the product itself, but rather, the features of the product. So, health supplements will always be popular, as people are forever looking for different ways to improve their health. What you have to decide is what form your supplements will come in. Protein and vitamin shakes used to be very popular, and sure, they still have their loyal customers, but what's trending right now are those shiny capsules and CBD oils. It would be smarter for you to start your supplements company by selling these types of products. Sneakers will never go out of fashion —well, not anytime soon. But the types of sneakers people wear in any particular season are what will decide the success of your business. Fashion is one of those industries where you can't be ahead of or behind on popular culture, but rather, you must be just on time. Maybe the sneakers that are trending right now are the very chunky ones. But something else you might want to take note of is the fact that pastel colors and whites are more popular.

You can find trends by simply searching for your niche on Google (you could literally search "current sneaker trends"), and scrolling through Images and Shopping. See if you can find any trends that pop up frequently. Next, verify your instincts by checking social media. Some of the celebrities and social media influencers should already be wearing them or using the products. We all know just how inspiring they can be, so the general public—your customers— will be looking for those products (or similar ones) soon, and that's where you come in. Then, depending on your business model (to be discussed in the next chapter), you will find the right suppliers to make or source these trends from.

The Importance of Brand Design

Choosing a brand name and working on your entire brand design (logo, slogan, colors, etcetera) can seem like an unimportant task for most people getting into the business. But the name and brand identity you set up for your business will instantly give consumers a certain impression about your business, whether good or bad—and you want to be on the good side here. Unfortunately, this does happen at a subconscious level, so you often won't be able to explain to people what your intentions are. If they like what they see, they'll be drawn to your business; if not, they'll be repelled by it, even if they can't articulate exactly why.

In terms of the name itself, one thing I've found in setting up some of my businesses is that all the usual names have been taken. A lot of people have started businesses within the segment you're looking to get into, so before setting up shop, make sure to research that the name you want doesn't already have a website domain or even social media accounts. You'll be pretty pissed to find out that your business name already has an Instagram account, for instance, and now you have to choose a different name for that particular account, and explain to potential customers that yours is GotchaGoodz with a Z, not S, unlike how it is on the website.

Pricing and Competition

Pricing is one of the things a lot of start-up owners stress about or get completely wrong. The first thing I want to mention under this section is that it's never ideal to compete on price. If the only value proposition you have for your business and products is that you're cheaper than everyone else, you're set to lose in the long-term, because anyone can come in and make their offer a dollar less than yours, and now you're left redundant. When considering the price of your products, you first have to ensure that the cost of making and promoting and fulfilling your products are considered when calculating the costs. Most people only consider the cost of production. So they say, "If it costs me $10 to buy one t-shirt, and printing a design on it costs me $3.50, then if I sell at a markup of about 50%, I make a profit because I'll be selling the t-shirt for $20."

What isn't considered here is the cost of getting the products to you, the cost of marketing the products on social media (you're most likely going to want to run ads), or the cost of your team working in the business together making the t-shirt come to life. If you're renting property and paying electricity to keep your Print-in-Demand shop open, you have to consider these costs too. The thing is, you can't tell what your competition's overhead costs are, so comparing prices alone to match theirs isn't going to count in your favor. As I'll show you later in the book, the best thing you can compete on is value. No one can provide the same quantity or quality of brand value as you can.

One last thing that I do feel is important to mention here is that a product that looks good can be priced higher based on aesthetics alone, rather than the quality of the product itself. You see this very often with beauty brands, but with electronics as well. The brand design or the general appearance of the materials will look pleasing, giving the consumer the impression that the product itself is good. Sometimes, they might even handle that electronic item with caution making it last longer—not because the product is good, but simply due to the fact that the user is more conscious about how they use it. Plus, if it was expensive, they wouldn't want to replace it anytime soon. So, spend some time on your brand design and the look of your products, because this can give you a price advantage that your competitors can't easily compete with.

License and Registration, Please

Registering your business name will allow you to open up a business bank account, and get a tax number for your business. This way, you can separate your personal and business finances. This will also help you sign up for third-party software and tools like the payment gateway on your online store. You can register your business as a sole proprietor, partnership, corporation, or Limited Liability Company (LLC). All the information on how to choose between these is freely available on the internet, and I want this book to be filled with useful information only. So, go do some digging, and see which one of these suits your needs and objectives —then come back.

Now, when it comes to most e-Commerce businesses, you don't need to acquire an online business license. Depending on the state you live in, a registered business is all you need to sell products both online and offline. If you're considering starting a marketplace like Amazon, however, you may be required to obtain a license, as you'll not only be dealing with the selling of your products alone, but others' as well.

Some Working Capital

It's a misconception that starting an e-Commerce business doesn't require any money to set up. You have to pay for the platform which will host your shop. Even if you're dropshipping, you have to buy some products to test out the quality. Unless you have a large network of friends and family that are ready to buy, you'll also need to pay for some advertising. You may also find that, to get better results, you need to first invest in software and tools, which will boost the appearance and functionality of your online store.

I always suggest that you start with what you currently have and work your way up, but be prepared to invest some of your own cash into your business. Then later, I'll share the exact amounts you might need. Now that you have your fundamentals sorted out, let's get your e-Commerce business set up.

The Start-Over

After several failed businesses, Vincent Campbell (Diesel, as his friends like to call him) wasn't sure if e-Commerce would work for him. He knew very little about the internet, except how to log in to his Facebook account, and how to scroll through the Apple App Store (mainly to check out the latest games). He'd be overwhelmed by the number of business apps available to the public, but didn't think he could leverage them to his advantage. A friend of his told him to go into e-Commerce: "Diesel, my man," he said, "instead of wasting your time and money on things that don't bring you wealth, you should go into business again—like, start an online store or something."

At the time, e-Commerce was already big, and shopping online, even for him, was something quite ordinary. Sure, you needed to be skeptical at times; there were big scammers out there, but for the most part, all the large online stores had been vetted by thousands of customer reviews and testimonials. Diesel had an understanding of what needed to be done to start a business, but wasn't completely aware of all the intricacies involved. He had a good assumption that starting an online business, for the most part, would require most of the basics that any other business would: Registration and some paperwork (all of which he could Google), some start-up funding (he had a decent paying 9–5 job, and if he could spend his money better, he'd have some to spare for a business), as well as a solid business idea (he had a few aspirations, but wouldn't personally think of these as solid).

Diesel's previous endeavors were in retail and restaurants. He loved food in particular, and his girlfriend would always say he makes the most splendid coffee. He knew if he'd give this e-Commerce thing a go, it would have to be something related to one of these passions. He read up on a passion-finder test first, which required him to:

1. List out 20-30 things he was passionate about (food, clothes, coffee, music, video games, and watching YouTube were some of the things that popped up on his list)
2. Find intersections between those things (although it was difficult, he got a few)
3. Circle three–five topics that are interrelated, and see if he could get curious about them (research them, listen to Podcasts and watch YouTube videos about them, talk about them with others without feeling bored by the topic, etcetera)
4. See if there's one topic that truly stands out for him (and to his slight surprise, it was indeed coffee)

Diesel and a friend owned a coffee shop once. It went reasonably well, but due to a mismanagement of funds, they went out of business when the COVID-19 pandemic hit, and they couldn't stay around long enough to keep the shop open while they weren't getting enough customers. It wasn't entirely their fault—no one saw the pandemic coming—so they never really planned for such a disaster. They owed the bank a bit of cash, so when they closed, they didn't leave with much of a profit. This certainly damaged Diesel's ego a bit. He's had other businesses fail before this, but he somehow believed that the coffee shop would be the one thing that worked out for him, and for a while, it did. But life clearly had other plans, and he had to go back to retail sales.

After a hefty pep-talk from his girlfriend, he decided to do some research on e-Commerce, and what would be required from him to set it all up. He researched the different products you could sell through e-Commerce and what was currently profitable, as well as the different business models you could run through e-Commerce, and even some digital marketing tips. Although he was great at sales, Diesel wasn't so skilled in marketing—let alone digital marketing—and he knew this would be a big learning curve for him. But, he was ready for it all.

Key Takeaways

If you haven't started your business yet, these are some of the things you have to consider:

- Do you know what products or services you'll be selling?

- What will the name of your company be, is it completely available for use, and is it a name that won't repel potential customers?

- Do you need any specific licensing to start the business, or do you just have to register it?

- Will you be registered as a sole proprietor, partnership, corporation, or LLC?

- Do you have a little money saved up to get started?

CHAPTER 2

e-Commerce Isn't Just Shopify but Niches Do Hold Riches

"90% of all Gillette Shavers are bought by women for the men in their lives." –Martin Lindstrom

It's an exciting time for businesses that have been in e-Commerce for years already. Due to recent global events, consumers from all walks of life—not just the young and financially affluent—are buying products and services online, and this shift will endure. The brands that have been around for years will take an even larger market share because the new customers will trust what the existing customers are saying about buying from these businesses. If you're new to the world of e–Commerce, you have a bit of catching up to do. Understanding your strengths and weaknesses in this space will be beneficial to your success:

- Don't expect large profits within the first 18 months. Unless you have a large marketing budget and can get world-class influencers to promote your products, lower your expectations of success while you're still learning the ropes. Setting your expectations too high, because you're comparing yourself to digital brands that have been around for 5, 15, even over 20 years, will only make you feel demotivated when you don't meet those goals.

- Do thorough research into your intended customers. Later in this chapter, I'll be sharing some details as to how you can do this. For now, you need to think about who you want your e-Commerce business to service, and what you can offer them that no one else is. This fits into the next tip...

- Be unique. There are thousands of individuals reading this book right now, planning their e-Commerce launch, and thinking about some of the same ideas that you are. Coming up with new ideas in today's world isn't always easy. Consumers already have everything they could need, or a solid alternative to whatever it is you were thinking of offering. Your products don't have to be unique, but your user experience, including how customers feel when they buy from you, has to be.

- Keep learning. The best part about being a start-up is that you can be agile and make a lot of mistakes, without it having a large impact on your brand reputation. Companies that have been around longer have systems in place which they've initially developed for automation and never got a chance to update with the moving times. As a start-up, you're still able to be extremely agile and make non-systematic business decisions, so you can grow even if you slip up along the way.

If you can dedicate the next two to three years toward doing just this, you'll find success in this booming sector. Now, there are several core business models you can use when selling physical products: You can have a specialized online shop, develop a marketplace, sell on other marketplaces, or do dropshipping. The business model you choose will ultimately depend on your resources, but also your business goals. Selling on the marketplaces others have developed won't enable you to establish a brand for yourself, for instance. Having a specialized shop, on the other hand, may limit your potential profits, and in order to grow, you'd have to expand on the types of products you're selling.

The Specialized Online Shop

Often labeled as the direct to consumer (D2C) model, a specialized online shop sells a select category of products to a specific target audience, like selling running shoes that you manufacture yourself (or perhaps pay a manufacturing company to bring your design to life). This model:

- Requires you to be highly brand–focused. You want consumers to recognize your name or logo as soon as they come across it. Setting up brand awareness campaigns will be of the utmost importance if you're a specialized online shop. Brand awareness can be done digitally through social media, and through more traditional methods like pop-up shops, where your intended customers can get a feel for the products, and if they like them, buy from the online shop (especially if you don't have much stock on hand).

- Cuts out the middle-man (hence the label D2C). You own all the functions of the business from design to manufacturing, to marketing and customer service. Your intended customers will get the opportunity to communicate directly with you. If they're not happy, they know exactly who they can talk to. Online shopping comes with a lot of problems, and mistakes are bound to happen. You could send someone the wrong size, or the incorrect product, resulting in them losing their trust in you. But this trust can be quickly rebuilt if you can handle the error fast enough. The middle-man, like a marketplace, dropshipper, or retailer, might not always be able to provide fast turnaround times when issues show up.

- Requires you to have a unique product or business model. There'll be plenty of companies selling the product(s) you do, and some of them are currently in large retail stores (and thriving marketplaces), so they're getting exposed to your intended customers, whereas you still have to drive traffic to your e–Commerce website. The only way you can do this is by having a unique, interesting, or creative offering for your customers. Consumers love what's novel but still familiar, so find a way to incorporate this into your brand.

The Pros and Cons

With a specialized online shop, you have a lot of control over every aspect of the business. This is great because you're able to identify problems quickly and resolve them as you see fit, but this also means more work for you. Consumers have come to like this D2C model, however, and find being able to build a relationship with the brands they love to be something worth cherishing, as this wasn't always possible in the past. So, you need to leverage this to the best of your ability.

Depending on your products, getting set up might require a large investment to manufacture the products and drive traffic to your website. This is because all business operations are handled by you, as the brand. Getting funding isn't always easy, especially if you're selling a product that isn't necessarily out of the ordinary. Making sure you've saved up enough money to get yourself running the business out of pocket, at least for the first six months, is something you should make note of. A lot of individuals think that e-Commerce always means fewer costs involved, and quick sales, both of which are only true under very specific conditions. Low start-up costs only apply to the dropshipping model, and quick sales occur for products that are in-demand, while super affordable.

Developing a Marketplace

A lot of the retailers that you'll find in your local shopping mall (and even the mall itself) act as marketplaces: They offer a wide variety of products from different suppliers and sell them under their brand. You can create a marketplace online using the same principle. This model:

- Requires you to source your products. Unless you have a lot of cash on hand, manufacturing a wide variety of products will not be ideal. In this case, it's best to source your products from different suppliers and sell them under your brand. Amazon acts in this way, and a lot of companies have tried to start marketplaces with the hope that they'll grow just as big. Chances are, though, that they won't be able to do so, at least not in the near future. Setting up a marketplace and managing hundreds of thousands of suppliers is a lot of work, and perhaps your marketplace should start with a couple of dozen suppliers, and work your way up from there.

- Will have you taking on all the problems of your suppliers. Customers won't go to the brands that produced the products when they receive faulty goods; they'll be knocking on your emails. Your brand's reputation is at risk, therefore, if you don't carefully vet the products you're offering your customers. A few bad products here and there won't be a train wreck, but if you (and your suppliers) keep providing defective goods, eventually customers will be annoyed and seek alternative stores to get their products. It's important to note here that one faulty supplier can affect your entire brand reputation.

- Will require you to be great at marketing. Acquiring this skill will give suppliers a very good reason why they should list their products on your marketplace, instead of hustling it out on their own. A lot of small brands haven't figured digital marketing out just yet, and would benefit greatly if your marketplace could run social media campaigns that drive traffic to your marketplace, and ultimately lead to conversions. I've seen many marketplaces that look like they're struggling to just post on social media; put simply, you can't afford this as a marketplace.

The Pros and Cons

The main reason why consumers love malls is that they can shop for a wide variety of products in one place, and if your marketplace offers that same feel, chances are consumers will eventually flock to your site. This does, however, mean that you would have to supply quite an extensive range of products and think of the shopping experience of your target customer. Consumers who are looking to dress up for the weekend will require clothing, hair care products, perhaps some personal care products, and possibly makeup, too. So, you have to plan for all the potential needs your customers might have, which can be very stressful for some.

With most marketplaces, you're only able to take a certain percentage of your supplier's profits and don't control the prices. Unlike shopping malls, most of your suppliers will most likely not pay "monthly rent," and so if you don't make any sales, you're essentially doing a lot of work for free, because you still have to market the products on social media and other digital platforms. You take on a lot of the financial risk, so you need to make sure that the payout is worth it. Some marketplaces venture into other secondary businesses as a way to make more money, and you might have to consider doing the same.

Selling on Other Marketplaces

If you're willing to share the profits, selling on other marketplaces is a great idea. The most popular marketplaces like Amazon and eBay will give you exposure to a wide variety of consumers, ready to make a purchase. Most marketplaces don't require you to have unique products or ones which you've manufactured yourself, so if you can find a reliable supplier for your products, you'll be able to get listed on a marketplace. This model:

- Gives you very little control. The marketplace will typically have a lot of regulations, terms, and conditions to which you have to adhere. This is to protect them (and their customers), so it isn't necessarily a bad thing, but it might require hefty paperwork, and providing product images and descriptions specific to their requirements.

- Requires you to develop multiple sales channels. You can't only depend on one marketplace for all your sales. Your customers will be hiding out on different marketplaces, just as they would be buying products from different retail stores. Try to get your products listed on as many marketplaces as you can. You may evaluate which platforms perform best, and switch out the ones that aren't getting you the results you want.

- Still requires some marketing from you. A lot of businesses selling through marketplaces expect the platform itself to do all the marketing for them. Push yourself to do some of your own marketing, and tell your customers which platforms they can buy your products from. If the marketplace is big, chances are your target customers are already buying from that marketplace, and never knew your products were listed there too.

The Pros and Cons

The biggest advantage to selling through a marketplace is getting exposure to a large number of consumers, who are all ready to make a purchase. Even if they're just browsing, they're browsing because they want to purchase something soon. Most consumers will browse through different brands before making a decision, so it would count in your favor if you already have some brand salience, and consumers recognize your company name among the brands listed. If you're in a marketplace where a lot of other brands are more well–known and have been marketing their products through other channels, you'll find it difficult to sell your products.

You also have to think carefully about prices. Just like in a supermarket, you'll be competing with other brands that are selling the same products you are. A lot of consumers look for the cheapest products, especially if the quality between products isn't that different. Look at your competitors, and be willing to dip the prices when necessary. Also, if you can just learn to write better descriptions, your products will sound better, and consumers might be willing to pay that extra $5.

Dropshipping

As mentioned, this is the most cost-effective business model you can start as an e–Commerce business. With dropshipping, you can sell products on your online store or marketplace without keeping any stock in a warehouse. This model:

- Requires you to vet suppliers. You don't have to keep stock, but you should ensure that the products you'll be selling are made from quality material, or at least that the quality fits the price. Buy a few products from each of your suppliers on different occasions, test the products, and check out how they handle deliveries, returns, and refunds. The last thing you need is having to deal with this when your customers are laying complaints.

- Makes you think carefully about pricing. It's easy to undervalue your prices as a dropshipper because you know you don't have to pay for warehousing or deliveries. You might also be worried that your customers will find the original items and complain that you've sold them at too high a price. One thing I've learned about business (and have seen from many business owners) is that your confidence in yourself determines your pricing. You also have to consider the fact that you have to maintain your website and pay for marketing and advertising, and if you want traffic to come and stay on your website, those two things have to be on point.

- Works great for all items, big and small. Perhaps you've had a business idea in mind that requires the shipment of heavy, fragile, or large products. These can be difficult to store, maintain, and ship, especially if you're just starting. You could include a dropshipping feature within your regular business, which allows you to sell the products that will make your customers happy, without physically stocking them.

The Pros and Cons

The biggest advantage of dropshipping, as mentioned, is that it has low start-up fees. The only fees you have to concern yourself with are the website setup and marketing costs (if you can find ways to market your products organically, even better). You may also need to set aside a budget for testing products. But this isn't always necessary if you've heard and seen good reviews about the supplier. You may also set up a virtual interview with them to ask some of your pressing questions, before proceeding with a contract. It's also a great way to earn passive income: You only have to set up the online store once, pay someone to manage transactions and communication between suppliers and customers, and monitor it monthly (or every other month).

This no-touch form of doing business isn't going to be great for everyone. Other people love having control over the supply chain of their products, either in terms of creation or just delivery. Some people want to have something to work on everyday and might get bored if they're not working on their business in some way. With dropshipping you should also consider building a brand for yourself. This isn't an easy feat, but it will keep customers loyal, especially as most of your products will be ordinary—very few companies with unique products feel the need to work with dropshippers, and would rather sell using the D2C model because this builds their brand.

Choosing the Right Business Model for Your e-Commerce Business

In an article published by BigCommerce, they mention that there are ultimately four questions you need to ask yourself when choosing a business model: 1. Who is your customer? 2. What resources do you have? 3. Which method is best for your products? 4. What makes you unique? Don't get stuck thinking about your next move for too long. Business, for the most part, is all about who's quicker, and who can get their brand out there the fastest. There's no doubt you'll make mistakes, but you can always learn from them, and even start from scratch. You can start with selling on marketplaces, then choose to develop your own specialized online store. The skills that you learned while trying the former will feed into your success with the latter. So, just get moving.

Top Marketplaces for Listing Your Products

You'll have to look at the rules for listing your products before you can decide which marketplaces you'll choose for your business because you might not meet the requirements for some platforms. Nevertheless, here are some popular marketplaces you should consider (in no particular order) according to E-Commerce Germany:

- Amazon: As America's largest online retailer, this is a no-brainer. With Amazon, you can choose which plan (free with per-sale fees, or premium) you'll be utilizing based on how many types of products you'll be selling.

- Walmart: This platform has been largely retail, and even after its move to e–Commerce, has only started accepting marketplace suppliers after 2016. This is a good marketplace to be on because the brand holds a lot of salience throughout the US.

- Best Buy: If you want to sell electronics, appliances, entertainment software, and home office products, this is where you want to be. If you get onto a marketplace that has a niche offering, the chances of your niche products selling are much higher.

- eBay: As Amazon's main global competitor, you may want to consider eBay, particularly if you're into retail arbitrage. Retail arbitrage involves you buying items at retail stores, and selling them at a large profit on the platform, even without a business license.

- Bonanza: This platform has a similar model to eBay, but sellers are only allowed to list antiques and unique products.

- Wish: Completely mobile, with hundreds of millions of merchants and customers across the globe, this is certainly a platform you'd want to get in on. Wish's biggest positioning is extremely affordable products for the everyday consumer.

● Facebook: For those who want to focus on social selling, the Facebook marketplace is a great platform. You don't need a business license to list products either, and it helps you make money by using a platform that houses 1.9 billion active daily users.

On Which Platform Should You Build Your Online Shop?

If you decide that you don't want to list your products on marketplaces, or want to build a website to support marketplace sales, there are a growing number of platforms you can use to build your website on, the two most popular being Shopify and Woocommerce. It's tricky to decide which of these two platforms is 'better' as they serve different needs, and work with different sets of skills and resources. Shopify is great if you have more money to spend, and with little technology experience needed, its drag-and-drop feature makes building a website easy. Woocommerce, on the other hand, is more affordable to set up, but isn't easy to navigate if you're not familiar with web design. A few YouTube videos can go a long way in getting you the answers you need, however.

In the US, Shopify owns 29% of the market share as it pertains to e-Commerce businesses, but Woocommerce isn't too far behind at 23% (Islam, 2022). But, this should give you an indication of what your current competitors and peers are using to build their e-Commerce businesses. I'd advise that you use Shopify if you'll be the one creating and managing the site. If you're able to pay for a web developer, perhaps going with Woocommerce might save you some money in the long run.

Finding Your Niche

Many people with minimum experience in starting a business have this idea that they don't need a niche because their products cater to everyone, or to a large group of people. Females between the ages of 20 and 40 don't count as a niche for your personal care beauty brand. Fortune-500 male CEOs in their 40s for your designer, formal footwear business is a better niche. The latter gets more specific about the characteristics of your intended customers and gives everyone an idea about the types of products you're selling, even before you mention them. This is what it means to create a niche; you need to get ultra–specific about who you want to serve, even if everyone can use your products.

Creating a niche for your business is also a great way to stand out and be unique. Plus, everyone who can identify with your niche will be drawn to your business and online store. Once they start using and talking about your products, others will also want to try them out (thanks to FOMO, short for "Fear Of Missing Out"), and you grow your brand from that. You can choose to dissolve your niche once you have enough people visiting your site and buying your products. But, to get started, incorporate these tips as you're trying to find your niche:

- Think about whether your products can serve any of the three main money-making topics people buy into (health, wealth, and relationships), and double down on that. If the answer is too obvious, know that just about all of your competitors will be doing the same thing. So, an online shop that sells yoga clothes and equipment will fall into the health category, and every yoga store right now will be sharing health tips with their intended audience, and working on ways to make more money as their customers become healthier. What very few people are doing is providing couples yoga information intended to bring them more love and connection, as they free their minds and uplift their bodies. This is certainly something you can look into.

• Do plenty of research into your competitors. Check out their websites, social media pages, ad listings, and even subscribe to their newsletters. This is how you'll get an idea of their niches and begin to think of what you can do differently. What are two words that describe your competitors, which you wouldn't want to describe you? Map out these words on a vertical and horizontal line. So, let's say most of your competitors sell expensive yoga equipment and make use of a wide variety of crazy, bright colors. Perhaps you can craft a black and white store, and source more affordable clothes and equipment.

• Be clear as to how you're able to help your customers in a way that no other business—and particularly no other competitor—does. What problems do you want to solve, and how can you solve them? What else do yoga practitioners want that they can't easily get elsewhere? The clothes, equipment, food, music, and exercise apps have been provided. Maybe you can have a quarterly campaign where your customers can celebrate being their opposite selves. Yoga practitioners are encouraged to be calm and zen; humble and healthy. No one would expect a celebration of anything other than that. But humans, being human, would appreciate such a gesture.

These, of course, are just examples. Yours don't have to be as crazy, but they have to be as creative. Your baby-clothes store can be something other than cute with pastel colors everywhere. You need to learn how to stand out and build a brand that others will want to be a part of. Don't be afraid to call out your customers and provide them with an experience that you know they want; not what everyone else is already doing because it's been working for the past ten years.

Creating a Customer Avatar

Part of deciding what your niche will be is deciding who your customer is. You have to create a customer avatar, which is, in the words of Customer Marketing Specialist Sydney DeVries, "a detailed profile of your ideal customer. It doesn't make assumptions or categorize people into groups. The avatar focuses on one person and outlines everything about them... [and] goes into much greater depth than a regular marketing persona" (2019). Your customer avatar has to be a map made out of:

- The roles your ideal customer plays. Are they parents? Are they in managerial positions at work? You need to determine this, as well as their demographics, like age, gender, income level, marital status, and education level. These are important, because a person's demographics influence their buying decisions. A mid-level manager with a family, for example, may want to dress formally and look good, but he still has to make sure he supports his kids, so an ad showcasing your expensive suits collection may not intrigue him much. On the other hand, someone occupying an executive role who can afford to spend a little more, and might feel like they have to so they could earn greater respect in their position.

- Their psychographics and interests of your customers. What do they enjoy doing on the weekend? Do they prefer Netflix and popcorn, or going to the movies with friends? Where would they like to go on vacation: A beach resort or a quiet cabin? You can then take this imagery and add it to your online store or social media pages, in between images of your products. The people that can relate to those images will be drawn to your business.

• Their goals and struggles. The reason people buy anything is to solve their problems or improve their lives. But, the same product can have a different utility in the mind of each user. That drill and toolbox you're selling can be someone's livelihood, and the next person's weekend hobby. Don't try and cater to all needs and goals, even though you can. Don't be afraid of saying that you have the best drills for DIY-dads. This doesn't mean you won't sell to anyone else, it just helps you position your brand better.

How to Source Your Products

How you source your products is closely related to the business model you choose, and even your customer avatar. Now, as much as you may want to follow your passion, you should also consider which products are currently trending and will result in faster conversions. A fun trick to use here is not to focus on the product itself (like a t-shirt), but rather, the style (colors, shapes, designs, etcetera) People will always need t-shirts, but the types of t-shirts they buy at any particular time will be in line with fashion trends, again, thanks to FOMO.

You can find out what's trending by scrolling through social media. Instagram is a popular platform where influencers show off their latest trendy goods, with the intention of getting their followers to emulate those trends. Pinterest is another great social app for tracking trends. Blogs, across a wide variety of categories, will share what's trending in their niche throughout the seasons. Finally, you may check Google Trends to see what people are searching for. Google Trends also lets you see if the searched-for terms are increasing or decreasing over the past couple of hours, 7 days, or

30 days. You'll be able to track if a demand for a certain product is increasing or decreasing, so you can prepare your business too.

Now, the three main ways people source products are through:

- White labeling and private labeling
- Wholesalers
- Designing and crafting

White Labeling and Private Labeling

Labeling, as the name suggests, is about putting your brand's name and/or logo on finished goods. With white labeling, you can get a bulk supplier of a product (like body lotions and shampoos) to send you a large supply of the products, then you put them into your smaller bottles and packages, and lastly, you place a label on these. Private labeling, on the other hand, involves getting a supplier to design and create the products you want—with your specific instructions—and putting them in packages for you. If you want to start your own line of energy drinks, for example, you could use this method. Both these options are also great if you want to have a specialized online store or if you even want to list your products on existing marketplaces.

Wholesalers

If you're searching for already manufactured and packaged goods, you can find them through wholesalers. Wholesalers provide retailers (offline and online) with a wide range of finished goods at a discounted price. You won't be able to brand the individual items, though, and you'll want to make sure the products meet your quality standards and the standards your customer avatar would expect. This is a great option for creating a marketplace. You can find suppliers who are willing to sell you a large supply of their products, and at a discounted price, so you can add a decent markup and make a profit. Some wholesalers are starting to offer dropshipping options as the need for suppliers for this business model keeps growing.

Designing and Crafting

If you're more creative, you can certainly choose to craft and design your own products like clothes or baked goods (the sale of perishable goods through online platforms is starting to increase). You're likely to source the raw materials for your products from wholesalers, and sometimes retailers, as well. I'd suggest you find wholesalers, as you'll pay less for the goods. People choose to buy from retailers when they're unable to find the wholesale supplier through a basic Google search or don't want to take on the risk of buying from an international supplier. This option is perfect for a specialized online shop and selling on marketplaces (maybe get listed on Bonanza if your designs are particularly unique).

How to Verify Suppliers

Regardless of the business model you choose, you will require suppliers, and you will have to test that your suppliers are who they say they are. Although the internet is an amazing platform, which has opened the world up to new possibilities, it has also opened up the minds of criminals to see more scamming opportunities. So, verifying your suppliers is a crucial step in your business planning. You don't want to get sucked into a situation where you receive money from your customers, you pay a supplier to fulfill the delivery, and they just go quiet on you. At the end of the day, it's your brand that's on the line, and people will view you as the scammer—not the supplier. So, the best way to verify that a supplier is who they say they are is to buy their products, even if it's a small sample, at least two times.

A friend of mine wanted to start a dropshipping company, and for those first few months, she tested out one of the suppliers she found locally. The first three or four times she bought their clothes, the delivery went smoothly. The third time, the delivery got delayed, and she had to go to the courier company herself to find her products. Turns out they were using cheaper couriers to save on costs, but this also compromised the quality of the delivery process. She gave them another shot, and bought a pair of heels she thought would sell well. This time, the item never arrived, and after over 20 emails back and forth over a period of three weeks, she managed to get a refund. This made her decide that perhaps dropshipping wasn't for her, and that she'd rather be in charge of the delivery of products. So, she started a specialized online shop instead.

This isn't to say all dropshipping companies are bad, just that you have to do some due diligence to avoid future problems once you start getting customers. If you aren't in a financial position to buy the products yourself, you can also contact the company that you're bringing on board as a supplier. Try and build some sort of relationship with one of the salespeople, or even the CEO of the company. People who are running scams don't have time to build relationships; they want to make quick moves and rip off people from a distance. You can also check reviews and customer complaints. Platforms like Aliexpress show you a supplier's 'feedback tab' where past buyers can either leave a positive or negative comment about them. If a supplier has more negative than positive feedback, you know this is a red flag. If they have no feedback at all, it might just be that they're new to the platform. You are then able to reach out to the supplier directly and ask them a few questions about the products.

Lastly, you can check forums and social media to see if anything pops up about a particular company. Consumers generally like to vent on forums like Reddit and Quora, a well as on consumer-driven platforms like Facebook and Twitter. Doing a bit of research on these platforms about a particular company can either bring up some bad stories or nothing at all, which—as I alluded to—isn't exactly good either, and requires you to do some further digging. Be careful not to allow the bad reviews to sway your decision, though. Bad reviews often shout louder than good ones, and often people who are happy with a product will just keep quiet about it, instead of leaving a positive review. Be sure to check the company's history, as well. There's just no way a company would be around for 5 or 10 years if they've just been scamming people this whole time.

Coffee for the Takers

Diesel knew that if he'd have to build his own e-Commerce website, he wouldn't want to give any power to anyone, as he just wasn't built like that. Although he wanted to create a marketplace where he could list a wide variety of coffee and related products, he knew he wouldn't have enough time to manage it all, and he wasn't ready to quit his job yet. The last option which gave him control, plus felt familiar to him, was creating a specialized online shop. He was still in communication with some of the suppliers for his old coffee shop, and could easily reach out to those he had lost contact with. He would start with three main categories: The coffee itself, the coffee machines, and the mugs.

Although he wasn't tech–savvy, Diesel found it easy to build an online store using Shopify. It took him a total of three and a half hours of watching YouTube videos, but he eventually got the hang of it. At $29 a month, he felt this was a great investment, and only needed to sell one bag of coffee beans to cover the price and still make a decent profit, even after Shopify's 2% transaction fees. Excitement boiled inside of him, as he finished setting up his online shop after about 12 days. There was a bit of stalling in-between on his side, and some days he'd come back from work too tired to work on anything. But, the bottom line is, *Coffee for the Takers* was fully set up and ready to accept sales.

Now, it was time to start thinking about the marketing for the business, and how to attract people to the website. In a blog he read, Diesel discovered that he first needed to think about the type of people he'd want to attract to his website, and to get super specific on a niche. Carving out a niche was a bit of a challenge, but he knew the type of customers he wanted to attract: They would be the same people that used to come to the coffee shop. Well, Diesel had one person in mind for the customer avatar. This particular gentleman didn't speak much, so Diesel had to speculate what type of person he was based on his demeanor.

He would come into the store, order one of three coffees (often depending on the time of the day, but sometimes just based on the look on his face), take a seat by a window table, open his laptop, and browse through whatever was on his screen. He always had a discerning face when he did this, so Diesel assumed he must be in an analytical role of some sort. He had a ring on his finger, and his stout shape represented that of the typical dad-bod. He only came in during the week, so he probably had a 9–5, one which really worked him hard. Diesel would sometimes strike up a conversation with him, as he would with most of his customers, and the gentleman seemed to appreciate Fridays, perhaps because that was his time to relax, watch a little sports—he mentioned an upcoming NFL game one time—and recover from the hectic week.

Diesel liked this customer avatar, partly because he could craft a unique niche from this, but still balance it out with the characteristics of a lot of the other individuals that walked into the shop. As it turned out, the shop was located close to a Business Park filled with workers from a variety of different industries. They all loved the premium coffee, and the coziness of the shop. Most of them looked highly professional in terms of how they dressed and typically carried themselves. Sure, now and then someone would walk in with joggers or shorts, but there was still something professional about them, like you'd find in a CEO on their day off. For the niche, Diesel liked the idea of being the premium coffee supplier for the career-driven people who can't start their day without a cup. He planned on refining this, as he'd continue working on his new business.

Key Takeaways

- There are four e-Commerce business models you can use: Building a specialized online shop, dropshipping the products of others, building a marketplace, and listing your products on a marketplace.

- Your business model of choice is dependent on your resources and objectives. Building a marketplace will be more expensive than just listing your products or doing dropshipping. Listing your products on other marketplaces means you have less control, and if you want control, then simply build your own store.

- Create a niche and customer avatar for your business. Research your competitors and create a niche different to them, but try to fit into one of three categories: Health, wealth, or relationships. Consider the demographics and psychographics of your ideal customer; what are their goals and struggles?

- There are three ways to source products: Through private labeling (very expensive) and white labeling, crafting and designing your own products, and bulk purchases from wholesalers (most affordable).

CHAPTER 3

Do It Once, Get Sales Forever.

"The hallmark of innovation is surprise. No surprise, nothing new. Nothing new, no interest. No interest, no value. Therefore creating surprise is a crucial step in creating value through innovation." – Marty Neumeier.

Yup. You heard that right. Forever. A sales funnel is a step-by-step guide that a business sets up internally to invite strangers to become paying customers. An evergreen sales funnel is one that works, all the time. Not everyone will find your website and make a purchase on that very same day, as some might get sidetracked and forget they were even looking at your products. So, you have to create a pathway for not only bringing customers in, but reminding them about your products consistently until they make a purchase. There are typically three phases to a sales funnel:

- The traffic source
- The offer
- Ongoing communication

Before I explain each of these in more detail, I'd like to emphasize that you should set up an *evergreen* sales funnel as you get started. This will save you some time and energy until you can afford to pay a team to run your sales campaigns for you. You may be tempted to set up a sales funnel around a particular holiday or event that your intended customers are interested in. Although this isn't the worst idea, you have to consider what you'll do when the holiday or event has passed. You'll now have to jump on the next event, which can get very taxing on your mind, especially as a start-up owner. With an evergreen sales funnel, you have to be as broad as possible, but still focus on your customer avatar's goals and struggles.

How you'd set up a sales funnel if you run a specialized store versus selling on marketplaces will be a little different, but as mentioned, just because the marketplace is supposed to promote your products, doesn't mean you can't offer a little helping hand and set up a sales funnel which leads to their website(s), or your product's page within the platform.

The Traffic Source

I won't go into too much detail right now, as the next chapter is dedicated to helping you understand the best traffic sources you can use to drive visitors to your website. For now, I just want to mention that the internet has made it possible for anyone to find their intended customers; you just have to be willing to find them. Social media, blogs, and podcasts are some of the best places you can find customers, and if you leverage these platforms efficiently, they'll help you bring in customers without you having to do too much of the work. The joy about sales funnels is that, much like building the website, you only have to create and set them up once. You may have to run a few tests, and ensure every phase of the funnel is optimized, but thereafter, it should be smooth sailing, at least for several weeks or even months.

The Offer

The offer refers to how you're going to get people to provide you with their email addresses or contact details, so you can be in consistent communication with them. Getting traffic can be quite expensive, so you want to move that traffic to a platform where you won't have to pay as much to tell them about your products, regularly. The offer you choose will be related to your customer avatar's struggles and goals. Now, your product doesn't directly have to be the solution here; if you sell graphic t-shirts with a 'global peace' theme for all the fun-loving individuals in the world, your offer can be a brochure on 'finding your inner calm,' because you know that this is one of the goals of your customer avatar.

"Sign up to our weekly newsletter for more alerts" isn't an offer. The ultimate goal is to get individuals to sign up for the newsletter, but you need to find a more creative way of doing this. Remember that consumers are bombarded with newsletters and newsletter requests every day, so you have to show them that yours is about helping them, not just sharing your products with them. There are two main ways you can set up your offer: Through downloadable information, or through webinars.

Downloadable Information

The internet is riddled with free information and content, but people love knowledge; especially if that knowledge can help them improve their lives or solve a problem they've been dealing with. As a platform that sells cooking utensils and kitchenware, the obvious downloadable information package would be an e-book with 101 recipes. But remember all your competitors are already doing this, so you have to get a little more creative, and that's also why you need to find your niche. Do a lot of your products have heat-resistant elements, making it safe for little ones to practice cooking with their parents? Perhaps a parenting cookbook or rulebook might work best for them. Do you offer utensils that save busy moms a lot of prep-time? Perhaps a time-management calendar might be useful to them.

Your downloadable information can come in a wide variety of formats, so don't just think of an e-book. According to business and marketing blogger, Mary Fernandez, you can use a:

- Cheat sheet
- Spreadsheet
- Full report
- Written tutorial or guide

- How-to video
- Template
- Calendar or planner
- Info-graphic
- Checklist or resource list
- Script
- Toolkit
- Quiz
- Printable quotes
- 30 day challenge

Webinars

Webinars have been around for quite some time now, but with recent global events, they've become more popular. Since we couldn't connect in person during the earlier phases of the COVID-19 pandemic, we became more accustomed to connecting online. Creating a webinar is a perfect way for you to connect with your customers on a personal level. Even if you don't do the webinar in person, and choose to create a recording instead, your customers will still appreciate that effort. Webinars are also a great way to build the brand of the business. Customers get to see some of the people who work behind the scenes, and again, that makes the experience of engaging with your business more special.

You can use a webinar to explain to customers how to use your products or some of the benefits of using them. If your products are unique and not yet being used by the masses, setting up a webinar to explain to your customers how they can leverage your products to make their lives better can certainly help. Now, let's imagine you've formulated the most amazing supplements for fitness geeks. Bringing these individuals into your world and showing them the benefits of your supplements in comparison to your competitors can also be useful. Plus, because the webinar would be more private, you don't come across as vindictive or 'competition-bashing,' as you would if you were to simply post about these comparisons in a blog or social media post.

Webinars can also be useful in training your affiliates about selling your products. Affiliate marketing is a great way to promote your products, but not everyone who would like to sell your products would have all the right information about them. Setting up an evergreen webinar giving affiliates a run-through of your products, and some tips on what they could say to their audience, will prove to be highly valuable to both you—as the business—and them, as your representatives. You also don't want a situation where an affiliate shares wrong information about your products, in an attempt to make more sales, so your webinar can explain the dos and don'ts they should adhere to.

Ongoing Communication

It's crazy how so many businesses neglect consistent communication with potential and even existing customers. If you want to be top of mind when your customers are ready to make a purchase, you have to put in the effort of communicating with them consistently. Communication can take place through emails, Facebook groups, and even phone messages. Then, there are three phases of communication you have to consider: After they sign up for the offer, regular newsletters, and when they don't buy anything.

Emails, Groups, and Messages

Ever signed up for a newsletter, or submitted your email address to a company (upon buying their products or for any other reason) and you get what you want, but don't ever hear from them again? This happens a lot, and I don't know how anyone can run a business without talking to their customers regularly. If someone agrees to give you their contact details (which can be quite tough these days), make the most of this. Email, although it may seem old-fashioned, is still one of the best ways to communicate with existing and potential customers. Brand consultant Katrina Kirsch found that "99% of email users check their inbox every day, with some checking 20 times a day. Of those people, 58% of consumers check their email first thing in the morning" (2021).

If you strictly want to use social media and have an active audience on Facebook, you can leverage Facebook groups and start a community-based communication system with your customers. The great thing about Facebook groups (at the time of writing) is that whenever you post in the group, every member will receive a notification (if their phone notifications are turned on) about your post. This isn't the case with posting on a Facebook page, though. On a page, only a small percentage of your followers see your posts. Building a group can be daunting, but it's proven to be advantageous for a lot of businesses.

The final form of communication, which has recently become more popular, is text messaging. In recent years, influencer-like entrepreneurs have encouraged their audience to send them text messages, and to keep in touch. This would be a great idea if you are to be the face of your company, and willing to work on your personal brand, in addition to your business. Of course, you can test it out even if you're behind a logo, but make sure that the information you share through this platform is more personalized and helpful, because text messages from businesses about their products aren't appealing to most consumers.

Phase One: Communication Post Sign Up

So, now that you have the contact details of your customers, you must maximize this opportunity. First, you have to send them the downloadable information piece you promised. But don't just leave it there; while you're still top of mind, and have just given your intended customers the best piece of information they could ever use, you're in a good position to make an offer about your products.

Set up a five-day communication sequence (or perhaps a video sequence—which would work especially well on the Facebook Group) where you:

1. Welcome them to your world, say thank you, and give them what you promised. Keep it short and sweet; the goal here is to have them download the information.
2. Explain how they can improve their lives even further; perhaps you can share a case study or your personal story. Don't focus on the products you're offering, but rather on the problem and results.
3. Introduce the product and explain the benefits of using it. Don't focus on the features of the product itself, but rather how those features can improve the life of your customer avatar. Don't link to the product yet. If you can get responses from people saying they want the link, even better.
4. Put your product on sale, and make the offer more irresistible by making it available for 48 to 72 hours only. You can also offer customers more value by providing them with further information they can download, or you can throw in an extra gift from one of the cheaper items you have in your product categories.
5. On the last day, simply mention what you have to offer again, then briefly touch on the benefits once more, and close it off.

Something rather annoying that I've seen many businesses do is put a time limit on their offer, then extend it after the time was supposed to close. This is sneaky and unprofessional. Stick to your word, as this also builds trust with your customers. If you want, you can always create a different sale, with different offers.

Phase Two: Communication Using Regular Newsletters

If your campaign was effective, you would have some people who bought your products, and others who didn't. Segment these two groups of people into different communication lists. You want to further personalize the experience of the two groups, and get the first group to buy more products, and the second group to buy their first product. So, you can't send an email with the headline: "If You Loved Our Denim Shorts, You'll Love These Too" if they haven't bought denim shorts from you. Your communication style to these two groups will be slightly different. This will be most effective if you're using email and text, and will be difficult to pull off when using a Facebook group. For the Facebook group, perhaps you can call out the customer segment you're trying to reach, by starting a sentence with: "To All of You That Have Bought Our Denim Shorts, Listen Up!"

Your regular newsletters should still be helpful, rather than self-promotional. If you're sending five emails per week, for instance, you can use a 1:3:1 formula. The first one can be a post/email/text where you're talking about your products; perhaps listing a new product, a product that sold out, or letting customers know about a current sale on certain products. Then, three posts need to be helpful: Style guides, recipes, checklists, etcetera. Anything that can help your customer avatar achieve their goals or minimize their struggles. Lastly, the fifth post of the week can be a company update, like a new blog, a feature in a magazine, or a social media post your customers might have missed. Just a note on the three helpful posts, though: This shouldn't be available to the public, like being on your blogs or social media posts (you can still hint at the tips you'll be sharing, of course), but you should make people want to sign up for that personalized communication, and find value in doing so.

Phase Three: When They Don't Buy

This might be difficult for some of you, but if after 12-24 months a person on your communication list doesn't engage or seem interested in your updates, and they've never bought anything, you can remove them from your list. Perhaps you can send a warning email saying "Respond to This Email/Text/Post If You Still Want to Be Here," and if you still don't hear anything from them, remove them. You want to be in contact with people who want to hear from you and are engaging with you. You're wasting time and money sending out communications to people who aren't interested, and perhaps too lazy to unsubscribe.

Having 1000 people on your list may feel good, but if 400 of those people aren't interested in what you have to say or offer, then in reality, you only have 600 people on your list. This means you actually have to work a little harder to get more people interested. Some people might just have joined in for that first offer, or they thought your offer could help them, but realized later that they were not exactly keen. So, always update your list and make sure your communication gets heard by your intended customers.

A Guide to Building Your First Sales Funnel

Now that you have an overview of what to do, you can start to think about the smaller tasks and concepts you have to bring together, in order to build your sales funnel. A lot of what I'll be sharing here is crafted from Russell Brunson's "One Funnel Away Challenge," which is a $100 program. I've taken it twice over, because it was so good, and I wanted to capture all of its information, use it for my businesses, and bring it to you. This is one of those pieces of information that you simply won't find anywhere, so do listen up, and perhaps grab a pen and paper to map this out for your business. I'll be taking you through a seven-step process for building your very first sales funnel, incorporating some of the elements you've learned above.

Solving Your Customers' Needs

Ask and answer the following questions:

- Who is your ideal customer? If you haven't done so yet, write down your customer avatar: Their demographics, psychographics, and struggles.

- What is the ultimate result they seek? Is it within health, relationships, or making money?

- What is the core result you want to bring to your customers? Think about the niche you're looking to serve and write down how you intend to help your customers. If you want to make them healthier, what are all the different health goals they would likely want to accomplish? Do they want to lose or maintain their weight? Are they looking to eat certain foods or cut back on others? Do they want to sleep better or just have clarity of thought?

- What can you offer? Bring it back to your business, and see if there's any health goal you can focus on, that's most in line with your business and products. For that yoga company I mentioned earlier, mindfulness and mental wellbeing are probably something that you can look into. Keep this in mind for that five-day communication sequence, but for now, you have to put together a front-end offer, like a webinar or downloadable information, allowing you to collect your customers' contact details.

Structuring Your Offer

Looking at the offer you've written above, break this down into smaller results you can offer your customers. Mental wellbeing covers a spectrum of topics from confidence to optimism to self-awareness. Which of these topics is currently on everyone's mind or is most appealing? Let's say you'll create *The Guide to Self-Awareness for the Frantically Minded*. This is what you're going to offer to your customers in the form of a webinar or downloadable information.

When presenting this to your customers, regardless of the format, it will be easier to follow if you break down the steps they need to take to get the result you promised, i.e., self-awareness.

Finally, Brunson suggests that the best way to teach your offer—again, regardless of the format—is by following these four steps:

1. Before you get into the details, explain how you learned or earned the information you're about to share. This helps your customers pay attention, because they know the information they're about to receive is highly valuable.
2. Go over the overall strategy. Briefly mention that there are three steps to achieving self-awareness, for example.
3. Go into the individual tactics. Under each of those three steps, there should be smaller steps or tactics—exercises, perhaps—which your customers can practice, helping them get the results they want.
4. Provide a case study. Nothing beats social proof; it's a great motivator to get people to take action on the information you give them. You want them to take action because when they do, they can see results, and they get to trust you even more. Your story, or the results of a celebrity/influencer, may count as social proof if this will be the first time you're presenting this to anyone. You would then like to ask your first stream of customers for their testimonials and update your information the next time you run this campaign.

Give Them No Reason to Say No

If you have more to give, give your customers more. Make it so that signing up is a no-brainer. A lot of your competitors are giving out free guides. So, you, too, should give out a free guide, as well as a checklist on things your customers should accomplish within the next 60 days as they become more self-aware, and a weekly planner to schedule their self-awareness check-in sessions. Remember that you also had the other mental wellbeing topics available, so perhaps you can add a report on how self-awareness leads to confidence. Throw in a free t-shirt, as well.

Don't be afraid to lose a little money upfront, if you know you can make it back later. The more you give to your customers—and they can feel or see the difference—the more they'll want to support you. You also have the option to put together a low-priced offer. In that case, when putting together the five-day communication sequence, you have a higher-priced offer. I've found that creating an opt-in offer, then requesting payment, makes it easier for you to capture your customers' contact details and try to sell to them in the future.

Creating the Sales Page

Once you're ready, you'll have to create your sales or opt-in page. There are several tools you can use to do this, like ClickFunnels or LeadPages. A sales or opt-in page, unlike your website, will only give your customers the option to sign-up (and perhaps buy what's on offer) or leave. They won't be able to see your whole website and anything else you have to offer, so you want to make this as detailed as possible, but still not too long that your audience loses interest. Most sales pages have the drag and drop function, and are easily customized to your needs and objectives.

The Script for the Sales Page

The final step is about putting your sales or opt-in page together. You can do a 'video sales letter' or use written words with some images. Video sales letters will be best, though, if you want to be the face of your brand and want to build a more intimate relationship with your customers. Neither is better than the other, however, and you should always focus on your business and your objectives. Here's what you should include as you're creating the script for your sales page:

- Introduce yourself, or the company. Share some important notes customers should remember about you, and give them a reason to want to listen further. If you were a yoga instructor before opening the yoga shop, this means you understand the needs of your intended customers. Keep it brief and relevant; this isn't the time to list all your achievements since grade school.

- What do you have to offer the reader? Is it a physical product or a piece of valuable information? Explain why they need this offer and in what ways they can benefit from using it. It would be advisable that you write these in bullet points, as people can take in information better this way. Whether you're offering a product, webinar, or downloadable information, you still have to focus on the benefits of the product in terms of how it can help your customers solve their problems. Don't only list the features of the products or the main headings you'll be covering in the material.

- Now it's time for your first call to action (CTA). Make it very clear how your audience will get the product or information. What do they need to do? Which details will they need to enter to get it?

- Increase the value of your offer by now including everything else you'll give them, if they sign up or buy today. Remember that you don't want to give them a reason to say no, so, if you now have more to offer—and still at the same price—this will encourage them to buy. If you don't have anything more to offer, perhaps this is where you can list out the main headlines of your offer, so they know just how much knowledge they'll be receiving.

- Your customer may be thinking this is some click-bait scam, especially if your offer is amazing. Reassure them that this is not the case. Don't shy away from the basic truth; you don't have to come up with some smart reason, and simply stating that you're looking to build your community can go a long way.

- Share customer testimonials, if applicable. If not, leave this detail out. You can give your customers a 30-day guarantee, especially for physical products. If they don't like the product or find that it hasn't provided them with the results you promised, they may return it; but very few people will. Even if they're not 100% happy with the results, most people will just let this slide, as they wouldn't want to complain about something they bought for less than $20—that would be a waste of time for most intelligent folks. But giving them that option shows that you have a lot of confidence in your products.

- Finally, recap the offer, the main result your customers will receive from it, all the other things you have to offer in this deal, and give the final CTA. This CTA should include simple instructions, like "download now," "sign up here," or "buy this,"—these all work well.

Copywriting Skills

Every inch of your evergreen sales funnel will require you to be convincing. You, therefore, need to work on your copywriting skills. Copywriting, fortunately, is one of those skills that always improve the more you use it. So, even if your first sales funnel isn't perfect, you'll eventually learn how to optimize it, for people to take action. Nevertheless, I do want to share with you some copywriting tips you can use to help get you started on the right note. You need to think about this as you build your sales pages, craft your emails, and post about your business on social media. I haven't spoken much about social media yet, and I will be covering it in great detail in the next chapter. If you want a more comprehensive deep dive into copywriting for online business owners, go check out the free course I talked about at the beginning of this book. Nevertheless, below are some copywriting tips you cannot ignore:

Have a Strong Why if You Want People to Buy

When someone comes across your content, they need to immediately know why they should pay attention to you, and ultimately buy your products. According to copywriting wizard Jim Edwards (I share some of the best teachings from him and other copywriters in my free course), there are ten main reasons why people buy (or buy into) anything:

- To make money. Ask yourself: What are three to five ways your offer can help customers make money?

- To save money. Can your offer save them money in the next week, month, or year; and if so, how much?

- To save time. Are you able to save your customers time, and what will they then be able to do with their time?

- To avoid effort. What is something your customers never have to do anymore, once they get your offer?

- To escape mental or physical pain. What is the pain your offer can eliminate, and what will this mean for other areas of their life? What would they no longer have to worry about?

- To get more comfort. What are three to five ways you can help your customers experience more comfort and convenience?

- To achieve better health by being more clean and hygienic (this one came as a surprise to me, but upon reflection, it was very true). How does your offer help them obtain better hygiene and/or cleanliness? How will this affect their overall health?

- To get praise. How will your offer make your customers the envy of their friends and family?

- To feel loved. Can your offer ensure that your customers get to feel loved? In what ways?

- To increase popularity or social status. Will buying your product or signing up for your offer result in them becoming more popular? How will this occur?

Different reasons appeal to different people. The same product or offer can make one person excited about the money they will be making, whereas the next one may just be buying it because they believe others will praise them for their newfound wealth, and still, someone else will just be happy to finally escape poverty and the embarrassment they've felt living with their mother past the age of

30. You can't include too many reasons in one message; this is why finding your niche is so important.

People Don't Care About You, They Care About What You Can Do for Them

This is why I mentioned that you should keep your introduction brief. You don't want to bore or intimidate anyone with your accomplishments. Instead, you want them to feel empowered, and make them know that you understand them. One of the biggest copywriting hacks you can use is to avoid using words like I, me, my, we, and ours. A lot of people will write something like:

> "Through my company, I have helped thousands of customers lose weight using my 4:2:1 rule and using the supplements we have on offer."

Even if someone wants to lose weight, this doesn't give them any reassurance that they will—because you're only talking about yourself, your company, and your clients. A better way to rephrase this could be to say something like:

> "If you want to lose 15 pounds in the next three months, all you have to do is apply the 4:2:1 rule and take these supplements. Thousands of customers before you have already done so and love the results."

Also, be sure not to talk down at your customers; don't make them feel stupid to make yourself feel smarter. Avoid using big words and technical jargon that only you and your team need to understand. Write and speak like you would if a friend wanted to find out more about your business, and you're walking them through all the cool points about it, and why you think people will want what you have to offer.

The Number One Copywriting Tactic You Should Learn Is Writing Headlines

Your headlines will be the predominant deciding factor as to whether or not someone buys your offer, or at least gives you their time. The headline aims to get your intended customers to stop whatever it is they were doing and focus on you, and whatever else you have to say. One of the best headlines you could use is telling your customers how to do "something" in "a short amount of time," without needing "anything else." For example:

"This Power Cooker will have you whipping up gourmet dishes for your whole family in less than an hour: No stove needed!"

Someone who loves good food but doesn't want to spend much time in the kitchen would love this. You may also ask questions in your headline, like:

"Tired of slaving over the stove for hours? What if I told you there was a better way to whip up gourmet dishes for your whole family?"

Asking questions makes the reader want to engage; they'll want to say yes to the first question, and ask how to the second. They won't be able to move past your content without getting their question answered. One last thing to note here is not to overdo it. Avoid words like "WARNING!" and "Perfect" in your headlines, as people are not that gullible, and may think of you as an over-dramatic internet weirdo.

Finally, you should consider creating hooks. A hook is a one-liner that builds curiosity in your audience. It shares a little hint about the rest of your copy but does not give it all away, so it makes customers want to read more. You can use the hook as your headline, sub-headline, or as the first sentence of your first paragraph. This is a story-telling technique, and stories always make for good copywriting and conversation drivers.

The Copywriting Formula That Never Fails

Working with copywriting formulas makes it easier to structure your writing so that both you and your customers can make sense of it. I'm sure you've read a piece of your work before, and thought to yourself, "Am I making sense here?" Chances are, if you have to ask that question, you're not. There are several copywriting formulas you can use for your content, but the one that's easy to remember can work for any business, and it just never fails to hit the right strings within your customers. I speak of the PAS Formula. PAS stands for problem, agitate, and solution.

So, you first want to call out and empathize with the problem your customer is facing. Next, you want to agitate on that problem and describe what would happen if your customer doesn't fix the problem, and continues going down their current path. Finally, provide the solution (your product or offer) your customer needs to use to ensure their future looks different.

Success Leaves Clues

Don't try to go at this on your own. If you still aren't clear on how you should structure your sales copy for any content you're creating, go check out what other people are doing. What are some of the emails you read that made you click and buy? What are some of the Facebook ads you've seen that didn't make you roll your eyes and scroll by? Have you seen an ad on Google lately that made you check it twice, just to be sure you read it right? Those people have mastered the art of copywriting. Study them and see if you can find any connections, patterns, and stand-out points among each of them that you can emulate in your business.

You can even check out what your competitors are doing. Is there something about their copy that's amazing? Incorporate it into your own, and if their customers like how their copy is structured, perhaps some of yours will appreciate that style, too. It's important to note here, of course, that you shouldn't directly copy anyone. Just see how they do things, and try to emulate those points; not the exact words they use.

A Funnel, But Not Just for Coffee

Diesel's first attempt at creating a sales funnel, as you can imagine, was an utter failure. He had no clue what he was doing, or how to structure it properly. He knew the basics: He needed to offer his products to his intended customers, and build out a single opt-in page that would be separate from his Shopify store. He spoke to his friend, the one who got him started, about his poor attempt at building his sales funnel, and the friend directed him to the OFA challenge. His friend explained to him that over the next 30 days, this is all Diesel should focus on; that it would be best if he put each day's tips into practice immediately, instead of doing what most people do, which is wait until after the 30 days are over, when they can have all the information mapped out.

So, Diesel jumped into it. He mapped out his customer avatar again; the result he knew they wanted was wealth. The core result he could offer them was financial freedom. Although Diesel's previous attempts at entrepreneurship didn't go so well, he was a fantastic salesperson, and he did have a knack for business and making money. Plus, with all the knowledge he gained from his bad experiences, he could bring those learned lessons together to teach his customers a thing or two. Coffee helped people stay alert, improved their memory, and made them enjoy their work more. Diesel wasn't yet sure how to bring it all together, but he knew there was a link here: Between his online store and the high-achievers he was targeting.

Nevertheless, he decided to create *A Five-Step Guide to Boosting One's Productivity*. Some of the information was taken from the internet, but also from personal experience. Coffee was obviously one of the tips, shared within the section on foods, drinks, and supplements. As part of the offer, Diesel would include a sample bag of one of the coffees that people used to love at his old shop. It was tough for him to do this, because this was actually the second most expensive coffee he sold. But Diesel knew that he'd have to spend a little extra to get the results he ultimately wanted. He'd make that money back by selling about 10 bags of coffee (because the sample size was only enough for up to three cups—just enough to get his intended customers begging for more). Also, he would only promote the sales funnel to people within his city, so he wouldn't have to spend much on delivery fees.

Diesel built out his sales page as outlined in the OFA Challenge, using ClickFunnels to build it out. He had used another sales page builder before, but he was amazed at the wealth of templates ClickFunnels provided—a little overwhelmed, too. He finally decided on choosing one of the video sales page templates. He was natural on camera, as his work required him to be talkative and put on 'performances' all the time. Plus, he wanted to be the face of his company. For the testimonial section, he asked friends and family who've tasted his coffee before to write him a short review, so he had more than 15 reviews to share, and ambitiously placed all of them strategically throughout the sales page. Less than halfway through the challenge, he was ready to get his customer avatar to sign up.

Key Takeaways

- A sales funnel is designed to collect people from a traffic source, show them your offer, and develop ongoing communication with them, until they make a purchase.

- You can find traffic through social media and other digital platforms, like blogs and podcasts.

- Your offer can be a free or extremely affordable information product (e-book, checklist, 30-day challenge, etcetera.) A free webinar is also an option (and is highly popular right now).

- You can develop a relationship with your intended customers through email (the traditional way never fails), digital groups and forums (you don't have much control here) and text messaging (also highly popular right now).

- Things to remember when building your funnel: Think about your customer's needs, make your main offer irresistible with additional offers (and perhaps a free product), and make sure your script is convincing—use emotion, share social proof, and make the benefits clear.

- Copywriting skills to remember for your offer, sales page, and ongoing communication: Have a strong why, make it about them and not you, pay meticulous attention to the headlines, and use the problem, agitate, solution formula. Check out the free course I put together for a deeper dive into the craft.

CHAPTER 4

Get Their Eyes on the Prize

"If you need to close your customer, you've done something wrong."
–Meir Ezra

The last step to bringing your sales funnel together is getting traffic to your sales page. Traffic simply refers to a large group of individuals who would be interested in your offer. It's important to go for quality over quantity here. Having 100 people look at and opt-in to your sales page is much better than having a thousand people see the sales page, but realize it's not for them. This is why it's important to have that customer avatar mapped out, because it will tell you where to find quality traffic. There are essentially two ways to get traffic: You can pay for it or try to get it for free (this is known as organic traffic).

This chapter will be exploring the organic and paid traffic sources you can leverage to drive traffic to your sales page. You can use more than one traffic source, as long as you'll be able to manage all of them. Remember that you want to have an evergreen funnel, where you only do the work once, with it then generating growth through automation, requiring minimum maintenance from you.

Organic Traffic Sources

Organic traffic may sound like a treat, but remember in life you always have to invest something: Your money or your time. So, organic traffic may be free, but to make it work for you, you have to put in quite a bit of your time. Some of the best ways to gain organic traffic are through podcasts, social media groups and digital forums, nano and micro-influencers or affiliates, and guest blogging.

Podcasts

No, you don't have to start your own podcast to promote your sales page. You can start a podcast for your business, but it may be a while before you gain a sufficient number of listeners who would hear about your sales page and what you have to offer. So, you should get on existing podcasts that already have an engaged audience. An article published by Buzzsprout (a popular podcast hosting platform) states that a third of Americans listen to podcasts regularly, and podcast listeners tune into eight different shows weekly. Podcast listeners tend to be more financially well-off, so they're highly likely to be willing to buy the products they hear about on the shows.

As a start-up owner, you might not be able to get on the most popular podcasts within your niche, and to save your ego, it would be best to aim for medium-sized podcasts that post weekly, which still have a large audience, and are already taking some sponsors. Having sponsors is an indication that the podcast has enough listeners that they can offer brands some return on investment (ROI). Search for the email address of the podcast you'd like to be on. Some of them will want you to pay to be a guest; say "No, thank you" to them. As a start-up owner with a great offer to present, realistic podcasters (not media platforms looking to make money at every angle) will gladly have you on board, and not charge you for your presence.

Aim to do at least one podcast interview per week. Your customer avatar will dictate which podcast shows you'll try to reach out to. It's pointless getting on a popular podcast that's all about cracking jokes when your target audience is more serious and concerned with personal development, more than entertainment. For these first few months, you'll have to do plenty of podcasts, but remember that some podcast listeners won't hear your interview until weeks later. Some may even discover your interview months later. The point is, you only would've done those interviews once, and those interviews—whenever people get to listen to them—will automatically drive traffic to your sales page months after you've done them.

Nano-Influencers, Micro-Influencers, and Affiliates

You may not be able to afford celebrity influencers to endorse you just yet, but you can reach out to nano and micro-influencers, as well as individuals who want to earn an additional income through affiliate marketing to promote your products. The influencers will need you to send them free products, and the affiliates will request a percentage of the sales they help you get. So, you'd use the former if your offer was free, and the latter if you'll be getting your customers to buy something.

When it comes to influencers, always vet them carefully: See that their personality matches that of your intended customers, and is in line with your brand. You'd want to make use of several different influencers at the same time, so your message can potentially spread far and wide. But you also want some of them to have overlapping audiences, so those audiences can be curious as to why two of their favorite influencers would be promoting the same brand. You can give influencers some direction about the type of content you'd like them to post about, but it's best to give them as much creative freedom as possible. Once you give them a script, it may come across as robotic, and you lose the magic you were trying to create in the first place.

Then, for affiliates, you'll have to provide them with some content material they can post. Blog banners, email banners, social media images, and their affiliate link will be some of the things they'll require to get them set up. You don't usually have to vet affiliates as vigorously, because they intend to provide value and make money, not just receive free products and grow their audience. Generally, affiliates tend to carry themselves more professionally.

Social Media Groups and Digital Forums

There are several digital forums (like Quora and Reddit) and social media groups (particularly on Facebook, but LinkedIn, as well) that have a large number of your intended audience. The tricky thing about these groups and forums is that you have to be helpful on these platforms, rather than self-promotional. People often post questions about the things they're struggling with, and your job is to find these questions, and respond to them (again, with a helpful tone; not to explicitly promote your offer). Starting your own group where you're able to post freely is an option, but it will take several months, maybe even years, before you gain enough members whom you could effectively promote your offer to. So, using an existing forum or group will save you time, but you have to respect their rules and conditions.

This strategy requires a little more patience than the previous options, but if you share enough helpful comments and replies, members in that group will eventually want to follow you, or you'll get the perfect opportunity to subtly respond with your offer. You can then send these members a link to your offer. The great thing about being on these groups and forums is that you get an opportunity to engage directly with your intended customers, ask them questions on how you can improve your offer, and get to hear about their struggles and goals, so that you can write better copy.

Guest Blogging

If the idea you've had in mind for getting traffic to your sales page involves the least amount of engagement with others, you could write blogs on popular blogs sites that you know your customers love to read. Guest blogging allows you to expose yourself to a large group of people within the niche you'd love to serve—again, without having to grow your own audience. It might be a great time for you to get into guest blogging, as according to digital marketing writer

Christopher Jan Benitez, "93% of editors stated that they plan on increasing or maintaining the volume of guest content that goes up on their sites" (2021).

As a blogger, you get to share your ideas and opinions around specific topics, but you might not always be able to talk about your business, products, or offers as openly as you would like. Blogs are meant to be objective, not self-promotional, after all. You are, however, able to share a short bio of yourself and the work you do. This is where you can invite people to sign up for your newsletter, or buy your offer. Not everyone that reads the blog will take a look at your profile, so this is another option that may require a bit of patience and work on your end. But if you don't mind the wait and you love writing, this is a decent organic traffic opportunity to look into.

Paid Traffic Sources

If you're looking to get faster results, and you want to be able to control the audience (to some extent, at least), then you can invest in paid traffic sources. Paying a platform to expose your offer to a large group of people may seem like the easy option, but there's much you'll have to learn before you perfect this craft. With organic sources, you don't have to (and for the most part, can't) concern yourself with marketing tactics, whereas paid sources need you to pay close attention to a lot of different elements. If you don't, you could ultimately end up losing more money than you're making. Some paid traffic sources you could use include Google ads, Facebook ads, Instagram theme pages, and macro-influencers.

Google Advertising

As the largest search engine, it's a no-brainer for most business owners to want to advertise on Google. Consumers generally turn to Google when they have a problem they'd like to solve or a product they want to buy. With high intent in mind, if these individuals come across your offer, chances are very high that they'd choose to opt-in or buy what you have to offer. The key to Google is to target these high intent keywords; they may be more expensive and have thousands of other marketers aiming for them, but they convert better. Someone looking for "running shoes prices" is more likely to be in the market for a new pair, than someone who just types in "running."

You can find high-intensity keywords (all types of keywords, in fact) by using tools like Ubersuggest. You can also type in "running" into Google search and wait to see what suggestions pop up, as some of these suggestions will appear due to previous things you've searched, but others are based on what other people typically search for. On mobile, (a lot of consumers use their smartphones to search for products they need) Google ads get displayed at the top of the page, as the first two to three websites are listed under the same or similar keywords. Here's a statistic you might be interested in: 70-80% of consumers ignore Google ads, and click on one of the first few organically ranking websites (Shelley, 2021). However, Google ads as a platform still make a lot of money, so they clearly do work, and will probably work best if you're able to leverage the copywriting skills mentioned in the previous chapter.

Facebook Ads

Although every social media platform welcomes advertising, Facebook ads are highly affordable and still prove to convert best, especially for e-Commerce businesses. As the largest social media platform, you're bound to find your audience on Facebook. You might have to do a little bit of A/B testing, but I've found that the key elements which determine whether or not your Facebook ads convert, are content format, audience, and the copy in the description. You may also need a little time on your hands, so give the algorithm at least three weeks to get in the 'groove' before you decide to completely give up on the platform.

I've heard many stories about how Facebook doesn't work and that Mark Zuckerberg is a money-hungry scammer, but when I asked probing questions, I found that they only ran one ad for less than two weeks, before deciding to scrap it all. Unless you have a magic crystal ball, you'll never win at Facebook ads (or at anything), if you don't test, refine, and invest in it. So, let's begin by selecting your audience. This is still one of the biggest mistakes business owners make as it pertains to Facebook ads. Facebook allows you to choose your audience's demographics and psychographics, yet most people only focus on the demographics and the niche. So, they'll say their target audience is single females between the ages of 25 and 34, who love fashion. The expectation is that selecting fashion, beauty, or any other niche and industry will attract people who are interested in buying those products.

Instead, Facebook finds everyone who's even remotely interested in those niches and shows them your ads, so even someone who owns a fashion boutique themselves will see it. Everyone who works in retail will see your ad, too. The better way to select your audience is by thinking of the psychographics of your customer avatar; which fashion brands are they interested in? Would they prefer Nike or Prada? Would they read Vogue or

Women's Health? Are there any particular TV shows they like to watch? Facebook won't have all the brands (especially those that are still up and coming), but they'll have most of the brands the average person would like. The more details you give, the better equipped the platform will be at finding your ideal customers— customers that love brands like yours, and are willing to spend on brands like yours.

Next, you want to focus on the content format. Facebook is one of the platforms that allows users to post whatever they want. Images, videos, text, GIFS, infographics, etcetera. You may be comfortable with using a specific format, but you have to test different formats to see what your audience responds to. Once you find that they prefer video more than images, for example, you can then test if there's a specific video (colors, graphics, or animations used) that your audience enjoys more. The final element you should test is the copy in your descriptions. Test different headlines, add hooks, switch up the bullet points, and see which CTAs work best. Eventually, you'll find what works for your audience and you'll be able to let your Facebook ad run for months on end, generating you an income while you focus on other things in your business and life.

Macro-Influencers

Different sources will give you different explanations as to what qualifies as a nano, micro, and macro-influencer. For me, a nano-influencer is someone with less than 10,000 followers, while a micro-influencer will have between 10,000 and 100,000 followers, and a macro-influencer has over 100,000 followers, but is not a celebrity (artist, actor, and other person in the media's spotlight). So, what makes macro-influencers so unique? Despite not being your typical celebrity, they've accumulated a large following on social media, usually around posting lifestyle content, but also focusing on a particular niche like beauty, fashion, fitness, or business.

Macro-influencers charge upwards of $1,000 per post because their word and endorsement hold a lot of value within the industry. Most influencers only collaborate with brands they love and recommend (some aren't as strict, of course) and their audience trusts that whatever they post about they're truly behind, and not just doing it for the money—even when there's money involved. Unless you have a large budget, you might not be able to pay multiple macro-influencers to endorse your products, but perhaps you could do a mixed approach where you have two macro-influencers, and up to ten nano and micro-influencers posting about your products, and offer at any particular time.

Instagram Theme Pages

I think this one requires a bit of an explanation: Instagram theme pages are both personal and business accounts that have generated large, engaged audiences around specific niches, without promoting one particular product. The account isn't necessarily run by an influencer either, as no one persona shares content about their life. It almost acts like a blog in which a wide variety of content gets posted, but still closely related topics get posted, too. Because Instagram is such a highly graphic platform which encourages the sharing of good products, these pages got into the Instagram game early enough to win over a large group of people and form a community around the products they can all love.

Building an Instagram account from scratch can be a lot of hard work, even if you are paying for advertising. Even though you may have to seriously look into it as your business grows, for now, you can request advertising space on these theme pages. You can send the account owner a direct message (DM) or email (if provided), asking them how much they'd charge you for an in-feed post (image or video) and a swipe-up Story or two. Calculate the price against how much Facebook would've charged you for a similar post (you can test this out in the Ads Manager dashboard before hitting publish. If their price is cheaper—and it usually is—use them. One more thing to note is that their engagement rate has to be well above 2%.

Coffee for the Takers, Taking It to the People

Diesel ultimately created a blended approach to his traffic strategy: 80% paid, 20% organic. He felt like he had to use Facebook advertising, as that was the main traffic source discussed in the OFA challenge. He also understood how easy it was, plus he already had a Facebook account and wasn't present on any other social media platform. Using his girlfriend's personal Instagram profile, they set up a business account for Coffee for the Takers, just to be present on the platform, and get a feel for it. In the meantime, he was testing out his Facebook ads. His friend advised that his ad budget had to be between $1,000 and $1,500, as a good starting point; if he was looking for conversions.

Diesel would've loved to do podcast interviews; he listened to a few podcasts himself and imagined how he'd respond if he was in the interviewee's seat. Unfortunately, there were no local podcasts in his city, and he needed something local, because he was only able to deliver the free coffee beans samples to people in his city. The next best strategy for him was leveraging micro-influencers. Together with his girlfriend, they researched the top posts and accounts under several hashtags, like #coffee, #coffeelover, #coffeeaddict, #coffeetime #specialtycoffee #instacoffee #coffeeoftheday #caffeine, and a couple others. Nothing came up for his city, unsurprisingly, so Diesel added his city's name as his hashtag, and a few promising leads showed up.

He reached out to these accounts with the proposal of sending them a whole bag of coffee (gulp), in exchange for 5 posts and 20 stories over the next month. They also had to mention the productivity guide and free coffee on offer. Diesel's girlfriend suggested that at least two of those posts had to be in the Reels format, as this was currently the best way to get a lot of exposure on Instagram. Eight of the accounts they had gotten in touch with agreed, and Diesel gave them total creative freedom, as he wouldn't even know where to start when it came to creating content around coffee for social media. For him, coffee was for pure consumption, but he knew that he'd eventually have to learn this craft.

On the other hand, his Facebook ads were performing reasonably well after two weeks of tweaking. He found that his audience responded best to the static images, rather than the animated videos he tried to create. Although the majority of Facebook users like video content, his audience—because of their characters—didn't want to spend too much time watching a video, and a plain image with a clear headline and CTA appealed to them more. Within three months, Diesel increased his ad budget from $500 (he didn't heed his friend's initial advice) to about $1,500 and saw a 4X increase in conversions. He couldn't tell if the increase was due to the increase in ad spending alone, because he had been working on refining his audience, too. Whatever the reasons, he was happy with the results.

He had built out his funnel completely: He had the ads running, and the micro-influencers promoting his offer. The ads were performing better, with only 1 in 25 leads coming from the influencers, even when some of those influencers weren't bringing in any leads at all. Upon signing up for the productivity guide, Diesel sent out a three-part email sequence: With ClickFunnels, he could send an instant thank you message and have his new customers download the guide, so he didn't need to send a thank you message via email. The email sequence consisted of a welcome email where he shared a customer testimonial, and over the next two days, he would accept payments for the whole bag of coffee beans. Because it was delivered locally, he knew all the people reading the emails would have tasted his amazing coffee by now, and would know if they wanted more of it or not.

Some part of him wanted to take things slowly, stick to his current strategy, and make as few mistakes as possible, but he knew that he needed to grow from this. So, Diesel quit his job (they told him he could come back at any time), and he started to focus on *Coffee for the Takers* full-time, thinking of all the different ways he could scale up.

Key Takeaways

- You have two options as it pertains to getting traffic: You can pay for it (faster results) or try to leverage free traffic (slower results, with a few exceptions).

- Four organic/free traffic sources: Being interviewed on podcasts; leveraging nano-influencers, micro-influencers and affiliates; sharing advice on social media groups and digital forums; writing guest blogs and linking to your offer through your bio.

- Four paid traffic sources: Google advertising, Facebook advertising, sponsoring macro-influencers, and paying Instagram theme pages.

CHAPTER 5

What to Optimize, What to Amplify and How to Scale

"The goal shouldn't be to make the perfect decision every time but to make less bad decisions than everyone else." –Spencer Fraseur

You have made it through the most difficult part of your journey. Getting started, and making that first sale is always the most difficult part for most. Everyone's journey will be slightly different because our skills are at different levels and the products we sell will be different, and have different demands. So, don't be anxious if you don't make a sale in the first month, when others are already raking in the big bucks. You just have to keep working on your offer, get to understand your customer avatar better, and keep practicing your copywriting. For your headlines, for instance, brainstorm between 15 and 20 headlines for every part of your funnel (the Facebook ad, the sales page, and the communication sequence), until you get the one that sounds best. Business isn't about luck, it's about how you leverage your skills and how much you're willing to work at improving them.

The final chapter will be broken down into three parts, each intended to help you increase your sales. You'll learn how to optimize your sales pages and e-Commerce website. You'll get to amplify your message and expose your brand to more people using more platforms. Finally, you'll learn what you can do to scale up and exponentially increase your sales, without necessarily working longer hours or selling more products. After all, the best kind of businesses is the kinds that run themselves.

Optimizing Your Sales Page and e-Commerce Website

Optimization is about refining what is already there. When you first start working on your business, the aim is usually just to get things set up. At this stage, you're not as concerned with aesthetics or creating a sales experience your customers will love. Now that you have all the basics set up, it's time to make your sales page and website look better and work more efficiently, so you can sell more products, and perhaps impress some of your customers that may need a little wooing before they can buy. People are different and respond to different things. Even though your customer avatar may be a certain way, you still want to cater to the people who don't meet all the requirements, but still fit into the fundamental scope of your avatar. You can optimize your business by working on upsells or one-time-offers (OTOs) within your sales pages, by continuously upgrading your copywriting skills, and doing SEO for your e-Commerce store.

Upsells and OTOs

An upsell is an offer you make to your customers right after they've purchased or signed up for your initial offer. Upsells work on the psychology of your customers, because someone who has just purchased or received one thing is more open, and in fact, wants to receive and buy more. This is why at the supermarket, they have small tasty snacks right at the checkout—even though you weren't planning for it, you just grab it on your way to pay. You can offer your customers upsells within your sales pages too: After they've signed up for your main offer, you send them to a new page where you offer them something else that's related to your main offer and business, and hopefully more expensive, or which can increase your total sales.

So, say your main offer is a vegan recipe book. Think about what else vegans would need to improve their lives (related to your business, of course). If you sell vegan-friendly groceries, this would be the perfect upsell. But eco-friendly pots and dishes also work well because vegans are typically concerned with the conservation of everything on Earth; not just animals. Even eco-friendly yoga pants will fit in well, too. Upsells work especially well when you use OTOs instead of evergreen upsells. With an OTO, you explain to your audience that this particular upsell or offer will only be available for a short period (between 48 hours and 72 hours works great). People respond well to urgency because they don't want to miss out (thank you, FOMO).

I touched on this previously, but don't position your evergreen upsell as an OTO. If you don't plan on removing your OTO after 72 hours or switching it up, don't say it's a limited-time offer. With software like ClickFunnels, you're able to incorporate upsells and OTOs into your sales page, immediately after your main offer. It's been found that you can use up to two upsells after any given offer —more than that will begin to annoy your customers. So, your main offer can be an extensive recipe ebook (remember you want to make your offer amazing) for $3. Then, the first upsell or OTO can be your eco-friendly pots for a ridiculously discounted price, like $97 for three pots, and they get the e-book for free. If they say no thanks, you just send them the e-book. If they say yes to the pots, you can give them the second upsell offer of receiving the e-book, the pots, and a set of your most popular eco-friendly plates and cups, all for $197. If they say no to this offer, just send them the pots and e-book, and thank them for their purchase. You can always offer them the set of plates and cups in another offer (make sure it's not the same as this one, though).

Continue Working on Your Copywriting

If you can master the art of using words to invoke the right emotions in your customers, there's no way you won't sell your products. Anyone who's currently struggling to make sales is most likely not paying enough attention to their copywriting. Sure, you might have to take a look at your products; perhaps find better suppliers, or get up to speed with the latest trends; but you should be able to sell at least one product to at least one person—even if it's just once—so long as you use the right words. Some additional copywriting tips Jim Edwards suggests include:

- Use storytelling. People respond better to stories than just descriptions and benefits. We're able to either see ourselves within stories, or the people we know. Within your copy, you can share stories about your personal life, your business, or the people in your life. You can share stories about the people you've helped by using your products, but make sure that the hero in the story isn't you or your company; that role should belong to the person who made that decision to get help and use the products. You can also create a story around how something was built. Instead of talking about your sneaker designs and how awesome or comfortable they are, what if you talked about your journey as you came up with each design? You could discuss what inspired you, what steps you took to bring the design to life, and whether you were met with any obstacle—how did you overcome it? This can be more inspiring, and perhaps even justify the cost of your sneakers if they're expensive. The final group of stories you can tell is about debunking myths, clearing up misconceptions, and/or correcting mistakes around your products or niche as a whole. What are some things people believe about olive oil that just aren't true? Are they using olive oil in the wrong way? How can they use it correctly?

- Add personality to it. People buy from people, or an idea about the people at the company. This is why companies, where the CEO isn't the face of the company, will still use a spokesperson, a celebrity influencer, or even a mascot to represent them. This is how consumers can decide if they like or dislike a brand or business. Some people want to start a faceless business because they don't want anyone to dislike them personally, and then in turn dislike their business. But, if there's nothing to like, and if there's no personality to your brand, people still won't buy from you, and you'll get the same (maybe even worse) results than from the people who dislike you. At least, those who dislike you may talk about you to their friends and family, and those people will want to go take a look to see if those negative comments were justified, so you inadvertently get more traffic. The best way to add personality to your brand is to have strong values and speak about them. Your values will determine how you do business and the types of products you sell. Those who can relate will stand by you, and everyone else doesn't necessarily matter—they're not your intended audience.

- What else can you do? You can always improve your copywriting if you just look hard enough. If your copy on your sales page, or any other platform, isn't getting you results anymore, or you're getting traffic but not conversions, find ways to optimize your copywriting. Start with the headline: Make sure there's a bold promise or benefit your audience can relate to. Look at the offer itself; make sure it's compelling, that it's clear what it's about and how it will help your customers achieve their goals. Using the PAS formula, drive emotion into the minds of your customers. Change the price, and test what happens when you remove the price (maybe your audience likes free things before they can make a purchase), decrease the price (low-offers below $10 can give some customers reason to buy, because they feel like the amount they'll be spending won't result in a big loss, even if your offer isn't great), or increase your price (some people look at price to determine value, so if your offer is too low, they think what you have to offer isn't that good). You may want to look at the colors and images you've used, as well. Some people react to different images and graphics in different ways. Colors also evoke different emotions in people, so make sure you're using the right colors as the background for your sales pages. Finally, get proof that your products work or that your offer is loved by others. Give samples away and make others read through your guide or report, and ask them for reviews. Social proof goes a long way.

SEO for e-Commerce

Search Engine Optimization, commonly known by its abbreviation SEO, is a marketing strategy businesses use to show up on the first page of search engines like Google. SEO is still one of the best ways to obtain organic traffic to your website, and as I alluded to earlier, it outperforms Google ads. According to news writer, Matt Southern, "The first organic result in Google Search has an average click-through rate (CTR) of 28.5%. Average CTR falls sharply after position one, the study finds, with the second and third positions having a 15% and 11% click-through rate respectively. Unsurprisingly, the tenth position in Google has an abysmal 2.5% click-through rate." (2020 July 14). So, if you ever needed a reason to want to do SEO, this might be it. If you can rank as the first (or at least third) organic result, anyone that searches for leather couches is highly likely to see and click on your website.

SEO requires a lot of work and patience on your part as a business, but the payoff is great. It can take up to three years before your business starts ranking on the first page of Google for the keywords you're striving for, because there will be other businesses fighting for the same keywords, with some already ranking for them, and there are several website elements you have to focus on, holistically, to optimize your website for search engines. SEO for e-

Commerce is different from that of content-based websites because the focus isn't only on keywords, but the product imagery and descriptions used, among other factors. In an article written by SEO expert and entrepreneur Neil Patel, he highlights all the different factors you need to consider for the optimization of your e-Commerce site, and I've broken them down as follows:

- Short-tail and long-tail keywords. Any SEO plan has to start with keyword research and selecting the keywords you want to rank for. You want to use a mixture of short-tail (designer sneakers) but also long-tail (designer sneakers for sale in New York) keywords. Next, you'll have to think about the intent of your customers, as they're searching for different products and solutions. Someone may be searching for a winter fleece, but in essence, they just want to be warm. So, even if you don't sell winter fleeces, you can aim to rank for that keyword, as the best winter fleece alternative.

- Product descriptions, images, and reviews. Your product descriptions should include keyword-rich information. If you want to rank for the keyword eco-friendly, this has to be present in all your product descriptions. You might be thinking that you've already mentioned it in your welcoming note, so your customers should know each product listed is eco-friendly, but Google doesn't care about that. Add CTAs in your descriptions as well, like "buy this now" or "buy our jojoba enriched shower gel." Again, this isn't necessarily for customers, but for Google to know that your website offers consumers the opportunity to buy something—and if this shows up in their search, Google will be able to refer them to your website. Besides making use of multiple high-quality images, you also have to ensure your images use the right keywords in the file names. People usually upload images using the file name on their phone or camera, and Google reads these as img00020220215.png, when you want it to read the name of your product or the keyword you'd like to use. When uploading images, also make use of tags, and create several tags using the keywords you'd like to rank for. Finally, encourage customers to leave a product review after they've made a purchase and prompt them subtly to mention the keywords you'd like to rank for within their reviews.

- User experience (UX). UX is about the design of your website, both in terms of how it looks and how it operates. You want to have a design that looks pretty, and includes the necessary images in all the right places—but you also want your website visitors to navigate the website with ease, and have them see images quickly. A site that has a beautiful image that embodies your brand, but takes forever to load, won't get you the results you were initially looking for. Another great tip for UX is optimizing your websites for both mobile and desktop use. Some websites look good on one but not the other, and your website must cater to both formats, because you'll have customers using both, with an increase leaning towards mobile. Don't pile images and words on top of each other because you want to fit as much content into a page as possible; a clutter-free website makes for better UX. Something else that improves UX are sitemaps, which provide visitors with an overview of your entire website, making website navigation much easier. Your sitemap should include all the product pages, categories, and blogs within your website, and allow potential customers to find what they're looking for without having to type it into the search—because sometimes they might not know the name.

- Rich snippets. Rich snippets are a piece of code you can add to your website (or through plugins, if you're using a platform like Shopify) that help Google organize certain information about your products. You can insert a product snippet, in which Google will extract the description and/or image and features of your products, and list them at the top of the search page. Ever searched for an HD camera, and got five or more images of cameras from different websites showing up, with their different features and prices? Those websites have added rich snippets. You can add rich snippets for images, features (like weight or dimensions), reviews, prices (and discounts), product availability, as well as videos. You can also do rich snippets for your business as Google ads, if you struggle to rank organically.

- Page speed. A slow website kills the organic ranking of your website because consumers aren't willing to wait for a website to load, and will leave a slow website. On the backend, what Google sees is consumers leaving your website, and assumes that your website didn't provide the consumers with the answer they required, so it decreases your ranking for other websites which can get consumers what they want, fast.

- Blogging. A lot of e-Commerce websites don't have a blog for their website. They find creating content to be tedious, but if you are serious about growing your business, you might want to consider creating a blog. It would be best if your blog doesn't talk just about your products, but rather, is catered to your customer avatar's goals and struggles. If you provide them with rich content which solves their problems, they start to see you as an authority figure, and not just another business selling products. Blogging also helps you with ranking for the keywords you like. There are only so many times, and in so many ways you're able to add keywords to your products descriptions. Plus, if you don't have that many product pages to add keyword-rich descriptions to, you won't be able to rank for those keywords with just ten products. You can make up for that with a blog, and you can have those keywords listed three to six times per blog, depending on the relevancy and length of the content or topic of the day. There's no limit to how many times a keyword can show up throughout your website, so why not use this to your advantage?

• Link building. You need to create content that links back to your website (backlinks); this tells Google that your website is credible, and that others find your content valuable. But, you also have to create internal backlinks, like linking products (when a customer buys one product they may want to buy something else that's related), as well as linking pages (for example, linking product pages to your blog posts, and vice versa). You can also link your blogs and products in social media posts, when applicable. Social media ads linking back to your website also count. You may do press releases and get featured in digital media platforms, or do guest blogging—as mentioned, they'll link to your business or offer.

Amplifying Your Brand and Business Operations

Amplification is about getting more people to know about your products and business. Most people will first test their business idea on a small group of people to see if the concept makes sense, to test out their skills, and to see if they're able to handle running an e-Commerce business before diving all in. But you can't stay small or localized forever, especially since the internet gives you so much opportunity to reach more people, and ultimately do more. Amplification is about going beyond brand awareness (where a select group of people know about you) into brand salience (when people first think about your business whenever they want to buy the kind of products you offer), then finally brand fame (where everyone knows about your products even if they never bought them—but it takes more than a decade to get to this point, so slow down, champ). There are several activities you can focus on to amplify your business, including brand building initiatives, social media content creation, and continuously working on your business operations and products.

Brand-Building Initiatives

The more confident you start feeling in your business, the more you'll be looking to share it with the world. Brand building initiatives will often cost you more money than what you're making back in the short-term, but the long-term benefits are worth the spend. The great thing about brand-building initiatives is that everyone can use them; you don't have to test which initiative will work for your brand, as all of them can. Some popular brand building initiatives include:

Freebies and Competitions

Everyone loves free stuff, and everyone loves to win. Many brands run competitions to grow their following and try to get more people to engage with their brand. The pay-off is that whoever wins (or the group of people who win) may become your new regulars if they love the products. You can also collaborate with other small businesses and have a big giveaway. This is great for businesses that aren't making that much money and wouldn't be able to run a competition alone. When you come together, the prize will be more compelling and you can each put in money for advertising. The last option you have under this category is simply giving away free samples or some of your least expensive items, so people can get a feel for your products and what you have to offer. Some might like them, some not so much. This also enables you to get some real-time customer feedback, so you can improve where necessary. Some businesses also give free samples to existing customers, which encourages them to try new products they haven't bought yet, and potentially increase their purchase value next time they buy something.

Branded Items

You can stick your company logo on just about anything, from office stationery to t-shirts to tote bags to coffee mugs, and even your car. The smaller items are what you'll be giving to customers, family, and strategic partners, and hopefully, their friends will become curious about your brand enough to ask more questions or do some online research. Try to be strategic about the items you put your logo on. A makeup store, for example, will benefit more by putting their logo on a makeup bag or toiletry bag and giving this to some of their regular customers (or when they purchase a certain value of products). Do you sell cookware? An apron or cute mittens can work. Are you in the business of automobile repair parts and tools? How about a car keychain? The more closely related the branded items are to your business, the easier it will also be for them (and more importantly, for others just seeing the items) to remember what your brand is all about.

Podcasting

Previously I mentioned podcasting, and being a guest on podcasts to generate traffic to your sales page. But, you can create your own podcast to promote your own business, in almost every episode. Podcasting continues to show growth year-over-year, and there's ample opportunity for you to get in, and get in front of your ideal customers. You probably won't get the results you want within the next 12 months, but a good piece of content eventually catches on. Want a podcast topic? Just think about your customer avatar and their goals and struggles. At the beginning of each podcast (or perhaps the end), you can let your audience know that the podcast has been brought to them by "your company" (you don't have to mention that you're the owner of the business).

Affiliate and Referral Programs

Better than trying to get affiliates to promote your offer, just get them to promote your products and your brand, in general. This takes a lot of the pressure off them to drive traffic and generate sales immediately and you can use their creativity to drive brand awareness. I'd also suggest that you run your affiliate and referral campaigns similar to how a network marketing company would. One of the reasons network marketing is so successful is because the members get trained and they have an opportunity to work like they run a company. People would prefer being and feeling empowered and don't want to feel like one of your little sales reps. Finally, the payout has to be worth it. Most programs only offer affiliates 8-10%

and as you can imagine, this doesn't motivate anyone to want to promote your products. Even if they initially do, they'll run out of momentum when they start to see that the amount of work they have to put in doesn't match the payout. Want better results? I'd suggest paying your affiliates 15% for large or expensive items, and up to 25% for smaller more affordable items. You should think of the lifetime value of the customers they'll be bringing in, and not only about the money you're "losing" (technically just sharing) now.

Influencer Marketing

Tech blogger, Tara Johnson, explains that "over 50% of consumers state that word-of-mouth and social media are their preferred ways to discover new brands" (2022). Most consumers don't always trust ads; the marketers and entrepreneurs that lie to and scam people have made it tough on the rest of us honest folks. But thankfully, there's still influencer marketing. Again, the idea isn't to get them to promote your offer, but rather, to help get greater brand exposure. Working with influencers on an ongoing (rather than once-off) campaign has proven to be more successful. Consumers can trust that the person really does use and/or like the brand and that it might be something worth buying. In terms of the type of influencers you use, just note that leveraging macro-influencers will help you grow your account faster, as their followers tend to be more open to following the brands the influencers share. There are currently companies that spend the majority of their marketing budget on influencer marketing, which runs far above a million dollars, and they're not making a profit yet. Of course, these companies have investors coughing up those large amounts of money, but they understand that investing in influencer marketing will pay off big dividends in the future.

Social Media Content Creation

The one thing I love about social media is that it's such a fair playing field for us entrepreneurs. Unlike with traditional media, the only thing that counts is how good your content is and whether or not you're able to build a community. How deep your pockets run is just a bonus—not a deciding factor of success. So, even the small guys get a fighting chance. In *Traffic Secrets*, Russell Brunson says something which I totally stand behind: "Showing you the strategy and tactics on one platform is the equivalent of 'giving a man a fish,' and teaching you the framework to get traffic from every platform is the equivalent of 'teaching a man how to fish'." (2020, p. 144). Although the four platforms Brunson and I choose to develop frameworks for are slightly different, and the frameworks themselves differ in detail, I stand by the idea of understanding the overall framework behind a social media platform, and applying it everywhere else you see fit.

The framework I'll be sharing with you is around content ideation and creation. I've had many people complain to me that they don't know what to create content on, and they're running out of ideas. Most of these people only think that they should be posting about their products and their business, so of course, they'll run out of things to say. There's only so much you can say about your business, and if you're starting with a small set of products, there'll only be so much you can say about your products, too. The key—I hope you've guessed it—is around creating content for your customer avatar, their goals, and struggles. So, the framework to use is called Value-Relate-Convert.

You want to provide value to your customers, you want them to relate to you, and you want them to convert into buyers. I originally used this framework for Instagram alone, but have found that it can be used for any platform, because on any platform you want to provide value, have your audience relate to you, and convert them into paying customers. You want to leverage all the features of any given platform, but this framework is particularly for the main feed of your social media platform of choice, because as a brand, this is what your visitors will be able to see when they come to your profile. Now, you want to be posting nine times a week (once, or sometimes twice a day), to make the framework work for you. For some of you that may sound daunting, or maybe even impossible, but I guarantee you: You'll be able to manage this with ease.

- So, on day one, you'll be posting something your customer will find useful, like a how-to tutorial.

- Day two, share something that you (and your customer avatar) struggle with. You want to keep your content light and entertaining on social media, though, so don't post anything too serious or depressing. A meme that talks about the struggle to wake up at 5 a.m. to exercise is relatable, entertaining, and a real struggle for most.

- On day three you'll post something valuable again; a tip you use to get the results you (or your customers) have achieved.

- Day four is something relatable again. A video or image of your workout room can be relatable to other home-workout fanatics.

- On the fifth day, that's when you post your first convert post. A post about one of your products will work here. If some of the valuable and relatable content has been leading up to the convert post, then even better.

- Day six is another value-driven post. Share three things (physical or mental) that you believe will help your customers achieve their goals.

- On the seventh day, you get to share something your customers can relate to, like a post where you explain your why, or some of the values you stand for as an individual and/or business.

- The eighth day is dedicated to more valuable content, like another how-to tutorial. Demonstrations or slides can help you walk your customers through the steps they need to take in order to get the results they want.

- Then, on day nine, you get to share another convert post. You may share another post about your products or direct your customers to your offer.

Instagram

This is one of the best platforms for e-Commerce businesses. Firstly, Instagram is a highly visual platform, so you can post pictures and videos about your products that stand out, and invite customers in. The brighter and more creative, the better. Secondly, Instagram is one of the biggest hubs for influencers, so you're bound to find individuals with a large following who share content around your products or something very similar. As mentioned, the Value-Relate-Convert strategy was initially formulated for Instagram and the 3x3 block of content which shows up when you view someone's account. Although you're able to upload a wide range of content, I'd suggest most of your content be 15-60 second Reels. At the time of writing, this is the only way to get a large number of people viewing your content without paying for ads.

Facebook

After a month of posting your valuable, relatable, and conversion-intent posts on Facebook, choose the three posts under each category that performed well organically, and run ads or 'boost' them at $1 a day each for 30 days. Each month, you'll continue to select your best-performing posts and boost them. There's no better way to amplify your brand on Facebook than by running ads. You can still apply the Facebook ads strategy highlighted in the previous chapter.

TikTok

This is one of the newest social media platforms, so organic traffic (again, at the time of writing) is still high. TikTok also has a growing number of influencers you can leverage, and this is currently how most brands are using the platform. I believe this is the best time for new businesses to build their brands on the platform. A lot of businesses aren't using the platform yet, and I've found that some of the big brand names (and the brands that were winning on Instagram) aren't able to 'win' on the platform without spending on ads or paying influencers. TikTok's users care less about brands and more about entertainment, so unlike Instagram, you can't just post gorgeous pictures of your products and expect a lot of views and followers. If you can get creative with this platform—right now—you stand to win big time.

Pinterest

I had to add Pinterest as the final social media app you should use as an e-Commerce business. It will be especially important if you have a blog, as you can drive traffic from the platform to your blog, seamlessly. Pinterest users, unlike other platforms, expect links to blogs. Having a Pinterest account also boosts your SEO while you're building your website's SEO. Meaning, if you're new to blogging, and try to search for your blog titles on Google, your website won't show up—all the other websites that have been doing SEO for those keywords will show first—but your Pinterest post with the title of the blog post will show up, sometimes within the first five search results. People can then click on the Pin, then the link to your blog and website.

Improving Business Operations

When you start your business, you're likely starting with some minimum viable product (MVP) in the sense that you only do the bare minimum to get you started, and to test your idea. Although we'd all love to, most of us will never get investors who are willing to fund our ideas, and we have to pay for everything using our savings or salary. It's okay if you can't pay for all the software you need to make your business run efficiently, but at this point in your business —now that you've tested the idea and you're trying to amplify your brand—you have to pay attention to even the smallest details which can help you improve your business, delight your customers, and ultimately increase profits. There are four key areas you can focus on to do just that:

Research and Development (R&D)

Take a look at your products; is there any way you can improve them? Can you add new product categories or variations your customers will love? Can you find better suppliers or cheaper suppliers that won't affect the quality of your products? Chances are you have to find local suppliers for your business, and can now look to source products from international suppliers, which will lower the overall cost price of your products. You can now also use the money you're saving to invest in other areas of your business. Spend some time developing your products and expanding and improving them, because your customers will love you for that. Plus, by now you should be crystal clear on everything related to your customer avatar, so you should be aware (instinctively or by listening) of what they'd like to see you do next.

Delivery

This is a key element that you can begin to optimize because there's a lot of anticipation around receiving products. Here are some interesting stats I found on deliveries, as published in Elogii (2020):

> "55% of shoppers in the US prefer same-day delivery to any other time of arrival. 58% of consumers don't want to wait more than 40 minutes for their deliveries to arrive. But, in general, nearly half, or 44% of customers don't mind waiting two days for their delivery to arrive. The reason is free shipping. 95% of consumers prefer free-one-day delivery as their ideal delivery method. 48% of customers will add more items to their shopping cart if it means they qualify for free shipping. Companies that add a free shipping threshold can increase orders by 90%."

If you haven't been doing same-day delivery, and offering customers free shipping, now is the time to do so. There's nothing more annoying than waiting for an order to arrive, and it can sometimes take forever. Your customers would rather just go to the mall when this is the case.

e-Commerce Automation

Right now, the only thing that's automated is your sales funnel (at least, I hope it is). Your ads and links should link to the sales page, which should instantly send through the offer (and have you notified if there's a delivery required), then your customer gets taken through the email or communication sequence. Again, you're notified if there's a need for a delivery. Now, there are other areas of your business operations that you can automate. First, I'd automate your content uploads. There are dozens of apps you can use to schedule content for all your social media accounts so you don't have to remember to post daily. You'll also want to schedule blog posts and have them run simultaneously with newsletter updates. Next, you want to automate internal communications, like receiving notifications about new orders, customer sign-ups, or when stock is low. You'll also require customer automation, like sending welcome emails, updates about orders and delivery, abandoned cart notifications, and review requests. Inventory management automation will also be helpful, as customers can be notified if they have to meet a certain threshold to buy certain items, or have products that are out of stock automatically removed from your site, then automatically re-added when back in stock.

Hiring the Right Team

Handling a few dozen orders is easy to do alone—or, well, it's manageable. But once you start getting hundreds or thousands of orders per month—and I'm assuming that's your intention since you're reading this book—you need to have someone (or a group of people) by your side to help you out. Always look to hire people who will share the same values as you and your customers. They don't have to work as hard as you, but they should have a strong work ethic, and be willing to serve your customers at every moment. You might have to consider creating a company culture, as well as a set of rules that everyone has to follow. Teamwork makes the dream work, and if anyone isn't willing to work as part of the team, don't drag out their dismissal.

Scaling Up for Unlimited Profits

Scaling up is about diversifying into other ventures so you maximize your profits. With your e-Commerce business running on auto-pilot and you having a solid team handling the day-to-day activities, and fulfilling your customers' orders; you can either use your money and free time to travel the world, or you can use the time and some of the money to set up opportunities for you to earn more money. Now, there's nothing wrong with choosing the former option. If you find your e-Commerce business can sustain you and your needs, there's no reason why you should go after higher profits. But I know some of you are searching for something bigger, and wouldn't be able to sit still on some blue-ocean island. Scaling up typically covers selling information products and monetizing your existing resources.

Selling Information Products

You've already had some practice with researching and putting together information products when you created your offer. Previously, the goal was to create something to give away to your intended customers in exchange for starting a relationship with them. There's so much you've learned about them and your line of business since the moment you started, and you can now take all your knowledge to put together information products to sell them for a profit. When it comes to the topic(s) of your information products, you can choose to provide more extensive information about your niche and your customer avatar's goals or struggles, or you can talk about your journey as an entrepreneur, and teach others how to do what you've done (like I do).

It all depends on where your passions lie. So, say for example you started the yoga clothing store because you practice yoga yourself, and wanted to create products that you and other yoga practitioners can find comfortable. Now, you can create an information product on yoga poses or how to incorporate yoga into your whole lifestyle, or you can talk about what it takes to design, source, and sell your type of products, so other budding entrepreneurs can do the same. There are plenty of information products you can create and sell, but the ones that perform best are books, online courses, and membership sites. Plus, these are great ways to earn passive income, because you only have to put in the hard work at the beginning phases, and they can generate repeat, monthly income for years to come.

Books

You can choose to create an e-book or a hardcover book. Most authors have both, in order to cater to different types of people. An e-book will be more cost-effective, however, and can be sold globally, with ease. If you want success with books (digital or physical), make sure that:

- The information provided is practical and useful. You can't just put together information and data that you find on the internet. The more personal the information is, and the greater depth of knowledge you provide, the more people will talk about your book, and word-of-mouth can carry it for you.

- You still apply the best copywriting practices in promoting and selling it. Just because you're a big-star entrepreneur now, doesn't mean people will flood to your virtual doorstep to read your book. You still have to convince them that this is the book to read and will help them solve whatever problem they have.

- You don't only market your book after it's been written. Tell people what's coming, so they can prepare themselves (and their wallets) for it. You can do a book tour (see, now you're traveling the world and making money) or get on different podcasts. As a successful entrepreneur, landing podcast interviews with the bigger guys will come easily. Put a team together, and go all out. You have to treat the marketing of your book like you would your e-Commerce store; you can't give less than 150% to it.

Online Courses

This is such a great way for you to bring your knowledge to the world. The popularity and use of online courses continue to grow yearly and show limited signs of slowing down. Ilker Koksal, a Forbes 30 Under 30 technology entrepreneur, says: "It's a fact that online learning is the future and will undoubtedly replace land-based learning in the future" (2020). As a transition from the business, your online courses can be about solving your customer avatar's problems on a deeper level. When putting together your online course, make sure that:

- You research other online courses to see what people have already created dozens of courses on, and how you can pivot. A platform like Udemy is very useful because you get to see the main lessons of other creators and emulate their structure, but change up your content.

- You plan multiple courses. You want to take your intended audience through a journey from beginner to advanced learner. Think of all the different steps you've had to go through (or you've taken others through) to get the results you're ultimately preparing your learners to achieve.

- You think about the distribution plan. Where will you host your online courses? There are several platforms available, each with a different audience and intention, but of course, you have to adhere to their rules, like any other marketplace. If you want more control, you can create your own learning academy through platforms like Thinkific and Kajabi, but this means you have to find your own customers, and can't leverage the existing customers on those platforms. A mixed approach might also count in your favor.

Membership Sites

A membership site allows your intended audience to experience a great volume of value from you, and pay a monthly fee. If you have a library of online courses, for example, you can turn this into a membership site, instead of having your customers pay for the individual courses. Other ways you can structure your membership site are:

- By building an app. A mobile application is a great way to get even more personal with your customers, and they'll have access to your information on the platform. If you want them to pay for it, you can't be duplicating material that's freely available on your blogs or social media posts; it has to be exclusive.

- Through offering exclusive training. This can work well for your affiliates. If you know some high-level marketing and sales tactics, you can offer these through a membership site. Your high-level affiliates, or the ones that want to learn more, can use this to build their skills and sell more products.

Monetizing Your Existing Resources

Instead of creating something new, you can look within your business to see which resources you can leverage to make more money. Making more money at times requires just a little creativity, and you don't have to start anything from scratch if that feels like a lot of work at this point. You can look to your assets or existing community.

Assets

If you have office space that you're not using (perhaps you had to buy a bigger building to fulfill more orders, but realize there's now too much space), you can rent it out to another business. There are always people in need of office space, and you can build new relationships and strategic partnerships this way. If you have delivery vehicles for your business and can fit in extra parcels, perhaps you can partner up with other e-Commerce businesses that don't have their own vehicles yet and make an extra few bucks just to travel the same route. Other things you can lease out include your office equipment and even marketing tools. Perhaps you bought a camera, tripod, and lighting to take pictures of your products, but don't use it every day; you can lease these out to upcoming entrepreneurs who can't afford their own equipment yet. Think outside the box and anything you own can be monetized.

Your Community

This is a little tricky because you don't want to be sending your email list to other businesses (this is, in fact, illegal). But, you can partner up with brands that have a similar intention to yours, and send a newsletter or two to your audience, about what they have to offer. You can do the same on your social media pages, as well. Remember how I spoke earlier about Instagram theme pages? What if you become the theme page (to a lesser degree, of course), and offer other upcoming brands the chance to advertise on your social media pages, as you already have a large and engaged audience? Finally, what about putting your podcast to use? That is, why not use it in other ways besides advertising your products? You can invite other brands to advertise on your podcast, and introduce products to your audience; ones you don't normally sell, but you know they'd find helpful. You can now become a media hub, not just an e-Commerce store, and there's a lot of money in media and advertising.

Will Coffee for the Takers Go Big?

The first chance Diesel got, he started a podcast. He was especially proud that he'd be the first podcaster in his city and hoped he could inspire other locals, and other people in neighboring communities to do the same. Keeping with the theme of helping career-driven men achieve financial freedom, the podcast would discuss some of his best tips for doing this. He shared his personal experiences, but also some ideas which he was yet to apply. In one of the podcast episodes about taking risks, he mentioned that I was the person who helped him get started; the one who told him: "Diesel, my man, instead of wasting your time and money on things that don't bring you wealth, you should go into business again, like, start an online store or something."

Yes, I was that friend! And I'm hoping that through this book, I can be that friend for you. Diesel's story, unfortunately, has to end here. I know you've grown to love him, but he's still in the process of optimizing, amplifying, and scaling; and perhaps I'll get to finish his story in the next book I write. Maybe I'll write about his story, and yours as well. I'd be honored to hear how you've applied the teachings in this book to take your e-Commerce business from just an idea to conceptualization, and on to earning higher profits. The e-Commerce space is only growing bigger, and you can be part of that growth if only you do the work. I'm not saying this will be easy; as you saw with Diesel, he had me on his side and still made errors (heck, I still make errors). He faced obstacles, but he overcame those with grit and a willingness to succeed. If you are willing, your e-Commerce business will thrive. But okay, enough of the sweet talk —let's go over the key takeaways for this chapter (I know I covered a lot) and close this book, so you can get to work.

Key Takeaways

- For increased profits you need to optimize, amplify, and scale up your business.

- Three optimization tactics: Upsells and one-time-offers; advanced copywriting; search engine optimization for your website (don't neglect product descriptions, get rich snippets, and start blogging)

- Three amplification tactics: Brand building initiatives (freebies, branded items, starting your own podcast, taking your affiliates and influencers seriously); content creation on Facebook, Instagram, Tiktok and Pinterest; improving operations (product development and expansion, faster and cheaper delivery, e-Commerce automation, and hiring the right team)

- Two tactics for scaling up: Sell information products (books, online courses or membership sites); monetize your resources (business assets or your community)

BONUS 1

The Action-Taker's Cheat Sheet for Getting Started

I'll assume that you've already registered your LLC Company and have set up your Shopify account for your dropshipping store. You know your suppliers, have a customer avatar, and are ready to jump into the world of digital marketing. This cheat sheet is for anyone looking to start marketing their business, and who is looking for a few extra pointers in the right direction, based on some of the things I've found work well for me.

Over the next 12 months, this is how your funnel can look like: Facebook ads > ClickFunnels video sales letter > First offer > Upsell (make it evergreen) > Five-step email newsletter. Now, let's say you sell home office equipment, furniture, and stationery to stay-at-home dads who run their own businesses. A weird niche, but definitely something that's happening more often with the global state of events.

The Facebook Ad

Image of a beautifully designed home office, but one that isn't as perfect as what you'd find in a female's home office. A white male in shorts and a rough beard is standing, facing forward with a smile and shrug, and he has a baby's bottle in his hand.

The headline: To all the stay-at-home dads balancing work and parenting, first of all, big ups to you! [Men love to receive compliments for something women have been doing for decades, so work with this. They'll want to hear what other compliments you'll be paying them]

Description: You've been pushed into a world where organization is key, and you know nothing about it. Calls from clients, meetings with your team, feeding your baby, responding to emails, yelling stop (while on the phone, and the person on the other end is so confused as to why you would ask them to stop), and finally, being thankful for 30-minute naps (not you; the baby). It can all be overwhelming, but there's a solution to the madness. I've created an organizational planner just for you. Now, you can organize your day around your work and baby's schedule, without loss in productivity.

[See how I worked in the PAS formula?]

CTA: Get yours in the link below.

The Video Sales Letter

As the CEO of the company, and perhaps a stay-at-home dad yourself, you'll be the perfect person to talk about your offer through video. After briefly introducing yourself, repeat the PAS formula that was in the Facebook ad. This reiterates your offer but also gives those who didn't read the whole Facebook ad to hear what you have to offer. It also allows those who didn't see the Facebook ad (but are, instead, coming from any other source) to know what you're talking about. In the rest of the sales page, follow the typical script outlined in Chapter 3:

Introduce yourself briefly. Some people won't watch the video, so you still want to write something like "Hi, this is Mike Stratton from The Furn Firm, I'm an entrepreneur and stay-at-home dad, whose life had been a chaotic mess until I discovered a few tricks which brought organization to what would usually be complete craziness.

The Main Offer

You'll then move on to discuss your offer and the benefits of downloading the planner. If you're offering the planner for free, you don't have to add additional tools to give away. If you're offering a planner (as in a physical board with an A3 planner) and you're charging a low price for it, provide some additional tools like a downloadable checklist, a free marker to write on the planner, and/or crayons for the little one. If you've helped other dads using your planner, share that. If not, share more details about your story, sort of like a before and after overview. Recap your offer, and explain how your customer can get a hold of your offer. Do they have to click the orange button to download it? Do they have to submit their details, personal information, and bank account, and pay through a secure online checkout? Don't undermine the value of explaining what will happen next. People want to be sure their online transactions—even if there isn't money involved—are going to be secure.

The Evergreen Upsell

For the upsell, if you initially had a free offer, your physical planner and marker can now be on offer. If your initial offer was for the products and a price, you can now throw in another item like magnetic bookmarks or stickers, and explain why these items will help your customer get to his goals, faster. You can make your upsell a one-time-offer, as this will drive more sales. This also means, though, that you have to come back to the offer every other day to change it. If you're up for the extra work and extra money, go all in.

The Five–Day Email Sequence

Remember, the point of the five-day email sequence is to sell another product. If your customer said yes to the free digital planner, but no to the physical product as the upsell, then in your email, you can explain how the physical planner will help them, and try to sell it to them once again. If they said yes to both, you'll now offer them the magnetic bookmarks and stickers. The goal is always to sell one more item that will help your customer get one step closer to their goals. Marketing automation tools will come in handy here because you'll be able to set up emails based on your customer's previous actions, so each new email will feel conversational rather than transactional. It would be embarrassing to send the same email to everyone, whether they've bought the upsell or not; it just wouldn't make sense. Now, you rinse, repeat, tweak, and improve.

BONUS 2

50 Profitable Niches and Products for Your e-Commerce Store

If you have no idea where to start, and are perhaps a little confused about your passions, that's okay. You don't have to have it all figured out to get started. Plus, I know some of you may have good ideas in mind, but are just looking for reassurance that you're on the right track. So, here are 50 niche ideas that are extremely profitable, and some products you can start selling within those niches. These aren't written in any particular order, so number 1 on my list isn't necessarily more profitable than number 50. Also, please note that the profitability of niches varies over time, do specific product research before going into each of these niches.

DIY Furniture

- Floating shelves (for home offices)
- Kitchen cabinets
- Entertainment units for the living room

Elder Care

- Supplements (if you can get licensed to store and deliver over-the-counter prescription drugs, even better)

- Warm and comfortable clothing

- Adult diapers

- Grocery delivery of healthy food

Gluten-Free Foods

- Cookies
- Pizza bases
- Baby food

Women's Fitness

- Light dumbbells
- Yoga mats
- Waist belts
- Scrunch-butt leggings
- Resistance bands

Superfoods

- Protein powders
- Supplement capsules
- Fruit or vegetable powders

Homemade Treats

- Candy
- Cookies
- Cupcakes
- Cakes
- Muffins

CBD Products

- Tea
- Chocolate

- Oils
- Capsules
- Balms

Organic Makeup

- Foundation
- Lipstick
- Eye pencils
- Mascara

Dog Products

- Dog costumes
- Grooming kits
- Dog food
- Carriers
- Chewable toys

Crochet Items

- Beach dresses
- Handbags
- Stuffed toys
- Oven mitts

Hair Care

- Hair growth oils
- Wigs
- Accessories
- Dry shampoo

Jewelry

- Friendship bracelets
- Fine jewelry
- Beaded jewelry

Denim

Can never go out of fashion...

- Jeans
- Jumpsuits
- Jackets

Culture-Based Meal Kits

- Italian cuisine
- French cuisine
- Mexican cuisine
- Chinese cuisine

Veganism

- Vegan replacements (veggies burgers, protein shakes, nut milks)
- Vegan baked goods
- Vegan-friendly makeup and personal care items

Gardening

- Potted plants
- Outdoor furniture
- Greenhouse kits

- Garden tools
- Seeds for fruits, vegetables, and herbs

Wedding Prep

- Dresses (bride and bridesmaids)
- Catering (large pots, dishes, champagne glasses)
- Wedding event decor
- Wedding presents

Baby Care

- Baby formula
- Diapers
- Teething toys

Video Gaming

- Keyboards
- Gaming chairs
- Consoles (PS5, Nintendo, etcetera)

Kids Clothing

- Princess dresses
- Superhero costumes
- School clothes (for private schools with uniforms)

Books

- Erotica
- Crime novels

- Kids' bedtime stories
- Autobiographies

Sports

- Bicycles
- Bats and balls
- Protective gear

Electronics

- Televisions
- Bluetooth headsets
- Blenders
- Multi-cookers

Home Decor

- High quality photo frames
- Vases
- Large rugs
- Farmhouse style wall decor

Alcohol

Requires a license as well, but makes for good business.

- Wines
- Whiskey
- Home-brewed beer

Designer Wear

- Sports (Nike, Adidas, Lululemon, Puma)
- Fashion (Balenciaga, Louis Vuitton, Gucci)
- Sunglasses (Ray Ban, Tom Ford, Marc Jacobs)

Face Skin Care

- Masks and exfoliators
- Serums
- Face cleansing tools
- Day and night washes
- Makeup remover pads

Home Gym

- Pull-up bars
- Treadmills
- Multifunctional trainers

Print-on-Demand

- Tote bags
- T-shirts
- Headwear
- Hoodies
- Coffee cups

Exclusive Toiletries

- Bamboo toothbrushes
- Activated charcoal toothpaste
- Leather toiletry bags

Packaged Healthy Snacks

- CBD gummies
- Matcha tea
- Keto chips

Male Grooming

- Beard oil
- Shaving cream
- 2-in-1 conditioning shampoo
- Shower gels
- Face masks

Lighting

- LED lights
- Ring lights
- Table lamps
- Chandeliers

Arts and Crafts

- Water paints
- Paint brushes
- Markers
- Canvases
- Scrapbooking stickers

Car Accessories

- Dash covers

- Seat covers
- Car stereos
- Air fresheners

Kitchen Gadgets

- Grape cutters
- Mandoline slices
- Pizza ovens
- Air fryers

Smart Home Products

- Smart speakers (Google Home or Amazon Echo)
- Door senses and locks
- Smart light bulbs

Undergarments

- Shapewear
- Lingerie
- Bras
- Corsets

Family Time

- Board games
- Picnic baskets
- Matching gear

Beachwear

- Bikinis
- Beach towels
- Embroidered cover-ups

Just Shoes

- Heels
- Sneakers
- Flip-flops
- Slip-ons

Camping Gear

- Tents
- Chairs
- Camping bags
- Inflatable mattresses
- Solar-powered batteries

Phone Accessories

- Tripods
- Car mounts
- Power banks
- Phone covers

Eco-Friendly Products

- Biodegradable diapers
- Metal straws
- Natural cleaning products
- Leisure wear

Household Cleaning Supplies

- Toilet cleaners
- Drain cleaners
- Kitchen counters

Circuit Boards

- For gaming systems
- For home appliances
- For navigation systems
- For security equipment

Dinnerware

- Rustic cutlery
- Vintage-style dishes
- Classic tableware

Computers and Related Products

- Laptops
- Keyboards
- Mouse pads
- Chargers and cables
- Wireless headphones

Home Comfort

- Electric blankets
- Fleece blankets with arms
- Seat cushions

- Space heaters

LGBTQI Community

- Gender ambiguous clothing
- Makeup for men
- Pride designs on household items

BONUS 3

The Tools and Resources to Grow Your e-Commerce Business

There are thousands of apps, tools, software, and other resources you can leverage to build your e-Commerce empire. Google is your first resource, and if ever you feel stuck in your journey, just search for it, I can almost guarantee you that someone has already been through it, and have the answer to get you to the other side. You don't have to use the suggestions I've laid out here, as there are always alternatives, but these are just some of my favorites, as well as the resources many others suggest.

Resources to Get You Started

Canva. A graphic design platform that helps you set up your business's brand design. $12.99 per month.

How to register a company:
www.nolo.com

Resources to Get You Set Up

Shopify. The most popular e-Commerce site builder in the US. Prices start from $29 per month.

Other popular e-Commerce website builders are Woocommerce, Wix, Squarespace, and Ecwid.

Popular payment gateways: Stripe, PayPal, Amazon Pay, Shopify Payments, and Square.

Popular marketplaces to list your products: Amazon, eBay, Bonanza, Walmart, Cratejoy, Best Buy, Houzz, Jet, Etsy, Newegg, Wayfair, Wish, and Reverb.

Popular Wholesalers: Manta, Wholesale Central, Doba, Chinabrands, WorldWide Brands, Dollar Days, Mega Goods, and

SaleHoo.

Resources to Set Up Your Sales Funnel

OFA Challenge. A 30-day challenge developed by ClickFunnels that helps you discover your niche, choose a product to start selling, and build out your first sales funnel. Priced at $100, with access to the membership site for additional online courses.

ClickFunnels. An all-in-one sales funnel builder that helps you set up your sales pages, upsells, email newsletters, and even membership sites. Price starting from $97 per month.

Other sales pages builders: Leadpages, Hubspot, Instapage, Wishpond, Wix, Mailchimp, Convert Kit, Kickoff Labs, and Unbounce.

Email marketing automation tools: Mailchimp, Convert Kit, Mailjet, OptinMonster, Hubspot, Active Campaign, and Salesforce.

Webinar hosting: WebinarJam, Webinar Ninja, Zoom, Google Hangouts, Get Response, Ever Webinar, GoToWebinar, and EasyWebinar.

Resources to Increase Traffic

Phlanx. Influencer engagement rate calculator (for Instagram, TikTok, Facebook, YouTube, and Twitch). Can also help you contact influencers and set up contracts with them. From $35 per month.

CJ Affiliate. An advertising company popularly known for linking businesses with affiliates.

Social media scheduling tools: Hootsuite, Sendible, Buffer, Plannable, Sprout Social, Coschedule, Falcon, and Loomly.

Resources to Accelerate Your Growth

Ubersuggest. This tool helps you decide on short and long-tail keywords you can use to optimize your website, but can also be used for blog suggestions. From $29 per month.

Shipping software to improve delivery: ShipStation, Easyship, Shippo, ShipIt, and EasyPost.

Recruitment Platforms: LinkedIn, Indeed, Workable, Zoho Recruit, Fiverr, and Upwork.

CONCLUSION

The End is Just The Beginning

"I have been through hell and back as an entrepreneur. If you're this passionate about what you do, you will be the person that stands out." –Forbes Riley

Building something meaningful takes time. I believe in taking action, fast—but not in rushing oneself when the timing clearly isn't right. How will you know when the timing is right? When the only thing you can think about is that one thing. People make time for what they prioritize. If something keeps "slipping your mind," it might not be a priority for you. You may be wondering, "what is Leon on about?" Why would I start my final chapter like this? The answer is really simple: I want you to build something meaningful. I truly love this industry, and I don't want anyone coming into this space with the intention to make money fast, rather than serve people. The advice I've shared in this book is extremely powerful, and anyone can use it to build a business—even if they don't believe in the business—and that's what I'm trying to avoid.

Anyone who applies the tips, especially those from chapters three, four, and five, now hold the power to sell any product, to anyone, regardless of the methods or small-time practices they choose. But the world is already filled with so many businesses that are just selling products for the sake of the sale. These people have mastered the art of selling and manipulation, without necessarily believing in their products or the work they're doing. Even if you are helping your customers, and providing them with the solution to their problems, it's not fair to them that your business is developed from a place of profit, not passion. In addition, these are the businesses that give up on themselves when they're faced with challenges. If you're not passionate about your work, you won't have the stamina to fight on when times get tough—and trust me, they will.

The Eight Rules of e-Commerce Success

Okay, let me get back to the practical stuff I'm best known for. Starting, building, and scaling a business has a very particular set of rules to it. If you follow these rules, you'll find success, and remember: You can't simply skip over the rules you don't like. So, I'll recap the important key points of this book as a list of eight rules you need to follow to find e-Commerce success:

Rule #1: Find your passion(s), and build from there. Regardless of what's trending or currently extremely profitable, this is critical. Trends come and go; your passion should travel with it.

Rule #2: Leverage the resources you have available to you for now. We all want to use the coolest, most expensive software on the market, but there is an alternative if you need to save money.

Rule #3: Are you willing to play by others' rules? Whenever you use the resources of others, instead of building your own, you have to play by their rules. Sometimes you don't have a choice, though, so get comfortable with doing things you don't always like. That's just how business is—especially in the digital world.

Rule #4: Know who you want to serve. When you have a clear idea about your intended customers, this will serve every aspect of your business (marketing and operations).

Rule #5: Communication is key. You have to communicate with your customers, before and after they've made a purchase. Be helpful when needed, and be convincing when the context calls for it.

Rule #6: You'll always have to invest something into your business. It may be time or money, but simply put, nothing comes free. Decide what you're willing to invest at any particular point; you can't always be throwing money at your problems, and you might have to invest the time to learn something.

Rule #7: Who you work with is important. Your team will either boost your business or bring it down. The purpose of entrepreneurship is to build something that others can manage, while you focus on higher-level tasks. If you're micro-managing everyone, growth isn't possible.

Rule #8: Growth comes from doing more, giving more, and thinking outside the box. Fail to do either of these, and you will remain stagnant, and even worse, your competitors will surpass you.

Knowledge Isn't Power, Only Potential Power

Power comes from practical action and putting your knowledge to work. This book, its value bombs, and all its resources will amount to nothing if you don't actually do what's written in it. So, go over the key takeaways and see what you can begin applying today. If you have to, go over the entire book once more. Make sure you take the free copywriting course at the beginning of this book as well. You'd be surprised how the same knowledge, read over multiple times, may have a different meaning and evoke something new in you. If you appreciate everything you've read and think this will be helpful to others, please do leave a review on Amazon. I wish you all the best in your e-Commerce start-up, and I look forward to hearing your success stories.

References

Benitez, C. (2021 December 05). The ultimate list of blogging statistics for 2022. Findstack.https://findstack.com/blogging-statistics/

BigCommerce. (n.d). Types of e-Commerce business models: Traditional and innovative new ones to consider.https://www.bigcommerce.com/articles/ecommerce/types-of-business-models/#selecting-your-ecommerce-business-model

Brooke, A. (2022 March 03). Podcast statistics and data: March 2022. Buzzsprout.https://www.buzzsprout.com/blog/podcast-statistics

Brunson, R. (2020). *Traffic secrets: The underground playbook for filling your websites and funnels with your dream customers*. Hay House Inc.

DeVries, H. (2019 September 25). What is an ideal customer avatar? Forbes.https://www.forbes.com/sites/henrydevries/2019/09/25/what-is-an-ideal-customer-avatar/?sh=55cab4f57327

E-Commerce Germany. (2022 March 16). 13 leading marketplaces in North America.https://ecommercegermany.com/blog/13-leading-marketplaces-north-america

Edwards, J. (2018). *Copywriting secrets: How everyone can use the power of words to get more clicks, sales and profits, no matter what you sell or who you sell to.* Author Academy Elite.

Elogii. (2020 August 10). 101 delivery statistics for 2020.https://elogii.com/blog/delivery-statistics-2020/

Fernandez, M. (2021 December 08). What is a lead magnet? 69 effective ideas and examples to use.https://optinmonster.com/9-lead-magnets-to-increase-subscribers/

Islam, I. U. (2022 March 04). Woocommerce market share: A comparative statistical evaluation. WebAppick.https://webappick.com/woocommerce-market-share/#:~:text=According%20to%20the%20latest%20report,%25%20and%202.32%25%2C%20respectively.

Johnson, T. (2022 January 11). Influencer marketing statistics for 2022. Tinuiti.https://tinuiti.com/blog/influencer-marketing/influencer-marketing-statistics/

Kirsch, K. (2021 August 13). The ultimate list of email marketing stats for 2022. Hubspot.https://blog.hubspot.com/marketing/email-marketing-stats

Koksal, I. (2020 May 02). The rising of online learning. Forbes.https://www.forbes.com/sites/ilkerkoksal/2020/05/02/the-rise-of-online-learning/?sh=32ee42fa72f3

Kutz, M. (2016). *Introduction to e-commerce. Combining business and information technology.* Bookboon.

Patel, N. (n.d). The ultimate guide to SEO for e-Commerce websites. Neil Patel.https://neilpatel.com/blog/seo-for-ecommerce-websites/

Shelley, R. (2021 November 04). 80 SEO statistics that prove that the power of search. SMA Marketing.https://www.smamarketing.net/blog/80-seo-statistics

Southern, M. G. (2020 July 14). Over 25% of people click the first Google search result. Search Engine Journal.https://www.searchenginejournal.com/google-first-page-clicks/374516/#close

Widjaya, I. (2020 September 04). Six business prerequisites of starting an e-commerce business. SMB CEO.http://www.smbceo.com/2020/09/04/6-business-prerequisites-of-starting-an-e-commerce-business/

www.ingramcontent.com/pod-product-compliance
Lightning Source LLC
Chambersburg PA
CBHW082109220526
45472CB00009B/2102